The COMMUNICATIONS HANDBOOK

SECOND EDITION

Senior Editor: Chelsea Donaldson

Nelson Canada
I(T)P An International Thomson Publishing Company

Toronto • Albany • Bonn • Boston • Cincinnati • Detroit • London • Madrid • Melbourne
Mexico City • New York • Pacific Grove • Paris • San Francisco • Singapore • Tokyo • Washington

I(T)P˜
International Thomson Publishing
The ITP logo is a trademark under licence.

© Nelson Canada,
A division of Thomson Canada Limited, 1996

Published in 1996 by
Nelson Canada,
A division of Thomson Canada Limited
1120 Birchmount Road
Scarborough, Ontario M1K 5G4

Printed and bound in Canada

3 4 5 6 7 8 9 0 /FP/ 4 3 2 1 0 9 8 7

Canadian Cataloguing in Publication Data

Main entry under title:

The communications handbook

2nd ed.
Includes index.
ISBN 0–17–604738–7

1. English language – Composition and exercises.
2. Language arts (Secondary). I. Title.

PE1429.C65   1995   808'.042   C95–931387–7

The Communications Handbook is based on a project originally developed by
Elk Island Public Schools, Alberta, formerly the Strathcona County Board of Education.

Executive Editor: Joe Banel
Project Editor: Carolyn Madonia
Senior Editor, First Edition: Paula S. Goepfert
Senior Production Editor: Deborah Lonergan
Design: Katharine Lapins
Cover Illustration: Wendy Grossman
Cover Design: Liz Harasymczuk
Composition: VISU*Tronx*
Input Operator: Elaine Andrews
Production Coordinator: Renate McCloy

REVIEW PANEL

Eldred Barnes
The Avalon Consolidated
  School Board
St. John's, Newfoundland

Rita Button
Edward Milne
  Community School
Sooke, British Columbia

Graham Foster
Calgary Catholic
  School Board
Calgary, Alberta

Kathleen Gregory
Sooke School District
Victoria, British Columbia

Hamish Guthrie
White Oaks
  Secondary School
Oakville, Ontario

Helen Hoey
Beiseker Community School
Beiseker, Alberta

Bill Hountalas
Durham Board
  of Education
Whitby, Ontario

Carolyn King
and the teachers of Elk Island
  Public Schools
Sherwood Park, Alberta

Bill Manson
Board of Education for the City
  of Hamilton
Hamilton, Ontario

Glen McColl
Crocus Plains Regional
  Secondary School
Brandon, Manitoba

Emmy Okazawa-Bortolin
Harry Ainlay High School
Edmonton, Alberta

Sylvia Unkovich
David Thompson Secondary
  School
Vancouver, British Columbia

Dirk Verhulst
Kenner Collegiate Vocational
  Institute
Peterborough, Ontario

Clevie Wall
Dartmouth District School Board
Dartmouth, Nova Scotia

CONTENTS

TO THE STUDENT

▶ *T*his book will answer your questions about a wide variety of every-day situations, both inside and outside the classroom: developing and presenting written assignments for school or work, conveying technical information, making speeches and oral presentations, working in groups, studying, writing exams, and many others. *The Communications Handbook* will be a useful reference in every school subject in which written or spoken communication counts. Keep it handy.

FEATURES

- As much as possible, the information is presented in the form of **lists** or **charts**, to make it more accessible.
- **Cross-References** in the margin point to other sections in the book that may be of use.
- The book contains numerous **models**, most of them written by students.
- Particularly useful or important **tips** are highlighted in coloured boxes found throughout each chapter.
- The handbook contains numerous **checklists** to help you apply the hints and tips to your work. You will also find suggestions for how to deal with writer's block and a troubleshooting guide to help you pinpoint what is wrong with a written draft.
- Each chapter includes some short exercises on specific topics. **Try It** exercises provide a quick self-test of whether you have understood a concept. The answers to these exercises are included at the back of the book. The **Apply It** exercises suggest ways to apply what you have learned to your own work.
- The **Index** is comprehensive and easy to use. As well, there is a **Table of Contents** at the beginning of every chapter so that the main topics covered are easy to find.
- A **Contents at a Glance** on the front cover flap and a **Quick Index** on the back cover flap provide easily-accessible reference points.

USING THE HANDBOOK

The handbook is designed so that you can refer to information as you need it, without reading through a whole chapter. Adapt the general tips and guidelines to your own individual needs. Here are some suggestions for how to use the book throughout the school year.

1. **At the beginning of the year:**

   - Examine the Table of Contents and Index, and then quickly skim each chapter. This will make it easier to locate information later on.
   - You may want to read through Chapter 8, *Study Skills*, right away. Its suggestions will be useful throughout the school year.

2. **Before you hand in an assignment:**

   - Use the Index or Table of Contents to find the section related to the assignment. Look over that section and any others that are appropriate to the topic.

   - For essays, research papers, and business writing assignments, turn first to the section on *Applying the Writing Process* at the beginning of Chapter 4, 5, or 6. If none of these chapters is appropriate to your assignment, or if you run into trouble during the writing process, you can turn to the general writing guidelines in Chapters 1 through 3 to find techniques that are appropriate to your work.

   - If the section you are reading has Try It or Apply It exercises, you may want to complete those before you do your assignment in order to check your understanding of the topic.

   - Use the checklists provided in each chapter to be sure you have covered all the important aspects of your assignment.

3. **When you get your assignment back:**

   - Your teacher may point out specific sections of the handbook that will help you improve your work. If so, re-read the section and do any Try It or Apply It activities to make sure you have understood the material.

   - Note any recurring problems on your own personal checklist, to make sure you catch them in future assignments.

THE WRITING PROCESS: TOWARD A FIRST DRAFT

▶

*E*verybody approaches a writing task differently. No one can tell you exactly what process and techniques will work best for you. However, having a picture in your mind of where you are heading is helpful, and knowing some tried and true techniques can get you over the difficult parts. This chapter will give you an overview of the stages of the writing process, along with some tips and pointers to help you find and limit your topic, define your purpose and audience, gather your thoughts, organize your ideas, and get your ideas down on paper.

CONTENTS

THE WRITING PROCESS: AN OVERVIEW

Few people can sit down and write well without some thought and preparation beforehand and some revising and editing afterwards. In fact, writing is really a process or a cluster of activities. The main stages in the writing process are prewriting, drafting, revising, editing, and presenting.

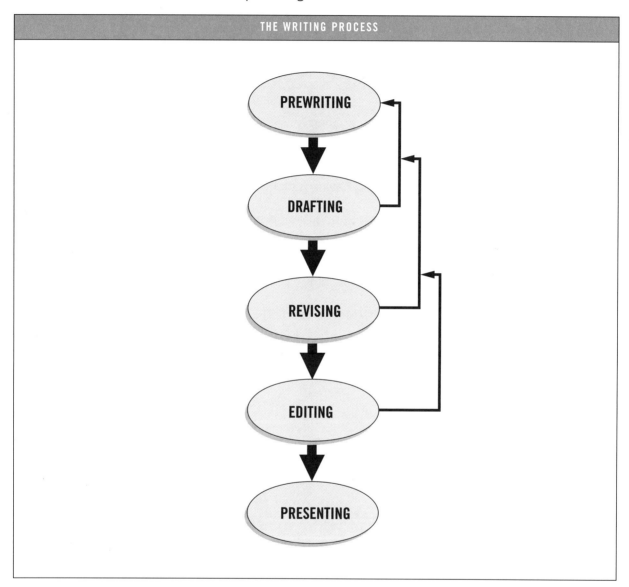

THE WRITING PROCESS

Writers tend to move back and forth among prewriting, drafting, revising, and editing activities. That is why the model has arrows pointing in both directions. If you find a specific way of working that suits you, then use it. However, if you don't know where to begin, or if you find yourself stuck at a particular stage, try some of the tips contained in this and later chapters to help you get going again.

Here is an overview of what happens at each stage, and the page numbers indicating where to turn for help.

STAGE	ACTIVITY	WHERE TO LOOK
Prewriting	Find and limit your topic	page 11
	Define your purpose and audience	page 13
	Gather your thoughts	page 13
Drafting	Organize your thoughts	page 13
	Write a first draft	page 17
Revising	Revise focus, structure, content	page 22
Editing	Edit paragraphs, sentences, words	page 25
Presenting	Proofread for spelling and punctuation	page 62
	Format final draft	page 83

PREWRITING

In the prewriting stage, you need to

• clarify your topic, your purpose, and your audience;

• gather information, ideas, and whatever else you need to help you write.

FIND AND LIMIT YOUR TOPIC

Here are some techniques you can use to help you generate ideas for your writing. If you are trying to think of a topic, begin by listing subjects that interest you. Then use one of the following techniques to generate specific topics based on those subjects.

METHOD 1: *Clustering*
Start with a key word or topic. Then write down words and ideas associated with the key word. Connect these ideas to the key word and to each other using circles and lines. Let your mind wander until you have exhausted all the possible associations. Here is a sample cluster using the key word "hero."

WORD CLUSTER

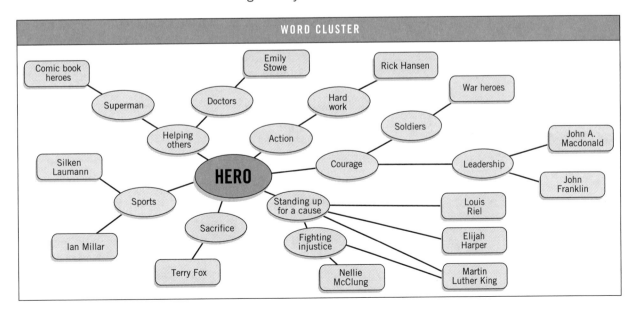

METHOD 2: *Freewriting*

As with clustering, you need to start with a general subject in mind. Sit down and write freely for a set period of time—say, five minutes—about that subject. At the end of the time period, look over what you have written and try to extract any topics or ideas that look interesting. One of these might make a topic for your writing, or you could try freewriting or clustering again, using the new idea as your starting point.

METHOD 3: *Brainstorming or Listing*

CROSS-REFERENCE

▶ See also *Brainstorming*, page 188.

It is best to brainstorm with a group of four or five people. You can brainstorm ideas for essay assignments, projects, or stories. Begin with a subject that interests you, or start from scratch and see what happens. Have one person in the group record all the ideas put forward by other members. Remember not to criticize any of the ideas as they are brought up. Your aim is quantity, not quality. Later, you can weed out the less useful suggestions.

METHOD 4: *Journal Entries*

Keep a journal over time to record your thoughts and ideas. When you need to find a topic for your writing, look through your journal until you find something suitable.

METHOD 5: *Reading*

The more you read, the more ideas you will likely come in contact with. If you are stuck for a writing subject, try flipping through magazines, newspaper articles, pamphlets, comic books, or any other written material. Even the pictures in magazines can give you ideas.

Narrowing an Assigned Topic

If your teacher assigns you a topic to write on, start from the assignment itself.

1. Look for a word or phrase in the assignment that identifies the general subject area. For example, if the assignment reads, "describe a baby-sitting experience you will never forget," the subject or key word would be "baby-sitting."

2. Use the key word to freewrite, make a cluster diagram, brainstorm, or simply list anything that is related to the topic.

3. Strike out any possibilities that do not interest you.

4. Look back at the assignment for other words that will help you limit your topic. Strike out any possibilities that do not relate to these words. For the baby-sitting assignment, you would have to consider the words "experience" and "never forget." Any writing ideas on your list or diagram that do not fulfill either of these criteria (i.e., that are part of a memorable baby-sitting experience) can be eliminated.

5. Consider which of the remaining choices you can cover adequately in the space you have available.

As a final check, ask yourself the following questions:

- Can I write about this topic in the time and space allowed?
- Does the topic satisfy all the assignment criteria?
- Am I interested in writing about this topic?

If the answers to all of these questions are "yes," you are ready to go.

DEFINE YOUR PURPOSE AND AUDIENCE

The clearer you are about your reasons for writing, the easier it will be to keep focused. There are many possible reasons for writing. Yours might be to describe a feeling or emotion, to share information, to express an idea, to entertain, or to persuade.

Your audience is whoever will read your work. Be clear about your audience's age, interests, knowledge, and expectations.

Once you are clear about your purpose and audience, write a one-sentence statement describing your topic, purpose, and audience.

> If you are writing for a teacher, assume he or she is interested in *how* you write at least as much as what you write about. However, don't choose a topic that bores you and think you can write well about it; your lack of interest will come through in your writing.

GATHER YOUR THOUGHTS

Next you need information. In a list or cluster diagram, write down all the information you have about your topic or idea: begin with what you know or think, then supplement this with more information. This may mean doing research on the topic, thinking through a scene or character in more depth, or backing up your ideas or arguments.

DRAFTING

The drafting stage consists of two activities:

- Organizing your thoughts; and
- Writing, writing, and more writing!

ORGANIZE YOUR THOUGHTS

Your goal now is to impose some kind of order on the information you have gathered. If you want to do a lot of organization beforehand, use both step one and step two. If you prefer to get right into the writing, and rearrange afterwards, you should still take a moment to think about the factors in step one. Then you can leave the outline or tree diagram for the revising stage.

STEP 1: *Decide on a Style of Presentation and Method of Arrangement*
Your presentation and arrangement should suit your idea, your audience, and your purpose.

Styles of Presentation Either use one or more of the following presentation styles, or devise another that makes sense for your topic:

- facts
- examples and illustrations
- specific incidents
- comparison and contrast
- cause and effect
- definition or description
- reasons or arguments

Methods of Arrangement Arrange your ideas in one of the following ways (or in any other way that makes sense):

- by time (chronologically)
- by importance or rank
- by features or characteristics
- by location or place (spatially)

How do you choose the right approach from all of these possibilities? There is not always one right answer to this question. Often, you have a choice of styles and methods. Bear in mind the following guidelines regarding possible arrangements, but don't treat them as hard and fast rules.

- Chronological arrangement may work if you are writing about someone's life or about a series of events.
- Descriptions are often arranged spatially or by feature.
- Persuasive writing is often organized from most important to least important (or least important to most important). Let the logic of each individual situation be your guide.

> If you are trying to persuade a hostile audience to accept an unpopular point of view, consider organizing your writing from least important to most important. That way, your readers will have your most compelling reason, example, or fact in mind as they finish.

▶ *In groups, or with a partner, discuss likely methods of arrangement for each of the following writing assignments:*

1. a newspaper story about a recent fire

2. a character sketch

3. a speech by a government official announcing the introduction of a new tax for consumers

4. a business report comparing two types of computer systems

STEP 2: *Prepare an Outline or Tree Diagram*

If you are very familiar with your topic, or if you are writing a short piece, deciding on a style of presentation and a way of arranging your information may be enough to guide your writing. If so, you can write a draft right away and finalize the organization at the revising stage. However, you may choose to go one step further and map out a more detailed path for yourself before you begin. Outlines and tree diagrams are two ways to do this.

Outlines An outline is a way of arranging your list of thoughts in accordance with your style of presentation and your method of arrangement.

1. Look over your list of information and try to separate the main ideas from the supporting ideas.

2. Decide which details to use to support each main idea.

> You will often find that one fact or detail will fit equally well in several different sections. Don't be afraid to try several different arrangements before choosing the best one.

3. If any of the points from your list do not fit under one of the main ideas, consider whether to cut them or to create another main idea. Ask yourself, "Is this information relevant to my purpose and audience?"

4. Arrange your ideas and details into the outline format shown below:

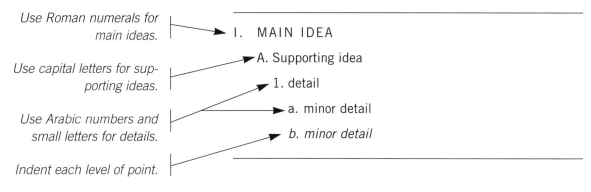

Use Roman numerals for main ideas. ➤ I. MAIN IDEA

Use capital letters for supporting ideas. ➤ A. Supporting idea

Use Arabic numbers and small letters for details. ➤ 1. detail

➤ a. minor detail

➤ b. minor detail

Indent each level of point.

5. If one of your ideas is not supported by at least two details, do one of the following:
    • Cut the idea out entirely,
    • Include the information under another idea, or
    • Find more supporting material to back it up.

Tree Diagrams A tree diagram is another way to show how your ideas link together. Put your topic at the top of the page, with your main ideas branching off from it. Then write in any supporting ideas and details on branches below each main idea.

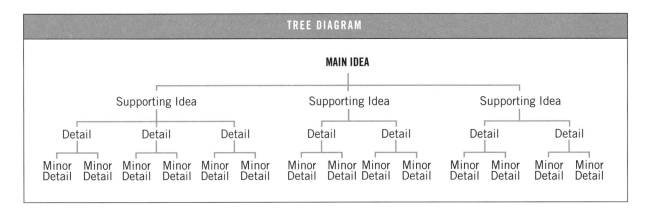

TRY IT!

▶ Make a tree diagram or outline based on one of the sample essays in Chapter 4.

PREWRITING CHECKLIST

Have I:

☑ Chosen a topic that interests me, that fulfills any criteria set out in the assignment, and that I can write about in the space I have available?

☑ Identified my purpose for writing and my audience?

☑ Gathered enough information, either from my own thoughts or from other sources?

☑ Decided on a method of arranging my information that is appropriate to my topic, purpose, and audience?

☑ Chosen a style of presentation that is appropriate to my topic, purpose, and audience?

☑ If necessary, prepared an outline or tree diagram to organize my information further?

WRITE A FIRST DRAFT Before you write your first draft, review the basic rules given below regarding general structure, paragraph structure, and tone. Don't worry too much about how the draft looks or about mechanics such as spelling, grammar, or format. Your main purpose is to get your ideas down on paper. You will have plenty of time to revise later.

> For the most part, these basic rules dealing with structure apply to non-fiction writing. If your writing is in another form, like poetry or narrative, check your library for a reference that will help you with the guidelines to follow for that form of writing.

General Structure

CROSS-REFERENCE

▶ Chapters 4 and 5 contain more specific information about the structure of essays and research papers; Chapter 6 explains the structure of business and technical communications.

- The beginning or *introduction* should capture the reader's interest and attention. It should also explain your reason for writing and give some indication of what readers can expect to find in the rest of the piece. (In some forms of writing, such as essays and research papers, this information is often contained in a thesis sentence. For more on how to write a good thesis sentence, see Chapter 4.)

- The *body* of the writing develops the theme or topic described in the beginning or introduction.

- The end or *conclusion* reinforces the theme or main idea, draws conclusions based on the details presented, calls the reader to action, or looks ahead to the future.

Paragraph Structure

- Write in paragraphs, and make sure each paragraph contains one main idea that relates directly to the main idea of the piece.

- Every paragraph should also contain a topic sentence, which explains the main point of the paragraph.

- Each sentence within a paragraph should relate to the topic sentence.

Tone The *tone* of your writing expresses your attitude towards your subject. In writing, as in speaking, your tone can be humorous, serious, light, satirical, sarcastic, sad, angry, friendly, etc. Compare the difference in tone between these two excerpts:

In the afternoon I was interviewed for the local TV station by a stiff-spined man in a tight suit. "What's this," he said, dangling one of my books nonchalantly by the corner to show the viewers that poetry isn't his thing, he's virile really, "a children's book?" I suggested that if he wanted to know what was inside it he might try reading it. He became enraged and said he had never been so insulted, and Jack McClelland hadn't been mean like that when he was in North Bay. In place of the interview they ran a feature on green noodles.

From "Travels Back," by Margaret Atwood. *Maclean's* January 1973. Maclean Hunter Publishing Ltd.

Lungren leads us quietly down the bank. "No quick movements. And don't talk; it disturbs them." I crouch on the edge of the water as four elephants come out from behind bushes on the other side. It is a moment suspended in time: the sun low and lunar, blurred by the dust, and these creatures dancing slowly, with trunk and ears and feet, steps stately, trunk movements exquisite, like the arms of Oriental dancers. They are just yards away across a shallow pond. One trumpets and runs a few steps toward the water. I leap backward. Lungren and the others laugh as the elephant turns its back.

From "African Deliverance" by Wendy Penfield. In *Best Canadian Essays 1990*. Saskatoon: Fifth House, 1990, p. 139–40. First published in *Equinox*, July-August 1990.

APPLY IT!

▶ *Look at each of the above passages and identify how the authors create the tone through sentence rhythm and word choices. Now look at works from your own writing portfolio. Note any techniques used by these authors that you would like to try in your own writing.*

Formality Writing can be more or less formal. Here is a paragraph written formally, along with an example of what the same passage might sound like if written less formally.

Formal: It is no use pretending there is no danger in climbing. Of course it is dangerous. The skill and the fun come from learning to recognize risk and to exercise a measure of control over it. Experience teaches a climber how to translate natural apprehension into sensible action, but above all to recognize the dividing line between acceptable risk and foolhardiness.

From *The Climber's Handbook*, Audrey Salkeld, ed. San Francisco: Sierra Club Books, 1987, p. 11.

Informal: Hey, let's not kid ourselves. Climbing *is* dangerous. Part of what keeps us climbers coming back for more is the thrill of recognizing what's risky and knowing how to handle it. Once you've got some climbing experience under your belt, you'll be able to translate your perfectly natural fear into a plan of action to get you out of danger. More importantly, you'll be able to recognize what risks are o.k., and what's just plain crazy.

- Usually, formal writing has a serious, factual, and impersonal tone and sticks closely to conventional vocabulary and structure.

- Informal writing, on the other hand, tends to be more familiar and friendly. It may include contractions and colloquial expressions and it is more likely than formal writing to be written in the first person and to address the reader as "you."

A P P L Y I T !

1. *Write a short review of a movie you have seen recently, first in a formal tone and then in an informal tone as if you were discussing it with friends.*

2. *Read a short story or article by an author you admire. Then write a fairy tale imitating that author's style. For example, you could try a version of* Cinderella *written in the voice of Holden Caulfield* (Catcher in the Rye).

Think about tone as you begin to write, but don't dwell on it. Once you have a draft to work with, you can look at your writing in more detail. Here are some final tips to get you started.

1. Start writing anywhere; it doesn't have to be the beginning.

2. Write in short spurts of five to ten minutes.

3. If the words are coming easily, DON'T STOP!

WRITER'S BLOCK: WHAT TO DO IF YOU ARE STUCK

Even professional writers write themselves into a corner sometimes. Here are some suggestions for when nothing seems to be working, or you can't think of what to say.

- Move on to another section.

- Write an opening paragraph.

- Look over your prewriting notes, clustering, lists, or whatever else you have done up to this point. These may remind you of what you want to say.

- Make an outline or tree diagram of what you have written so far.

- Doodle or draw a sketch of what you want to say.

- Complete the following sentence: "What I really mean to say is...."

- Find a willing listener, and explain to him or her what you are trying to say. Explaining your purpose to an outsider can help to clarify it for yourself.

- Show your writing to someone else. Ask them to comment on it and ask you questions about it that they have.

- If all else fails, leave your writing aside for a few hours or, if possible, overnight. When you come back to the task, your thoughts will probably be clearer.

IMPROVING A DRAFT: REVISING AND EDITING

▶ **O**nce you have written a draft, there is still a lot of work to do before it will be ready to hand in. Use this chapter as a guide to revising and editing your writing. It gives a step by step approach to improving your work, starting with revisions to focus, organization, and content, and moving on to a closer look at paragraphs, sentences, and words.

CONTENTS

REVISING
REVISE YOUR DRAFT

CROSS-REFERENCE

▶ The chart given on page 11 shows how revising and editing fit into the writing process.

When you revise your draft, you don't have to fix everything at once, but you do have to fix the hard things first, namely:

• Focus. Does it address your audience and fulfill your purpose?

• Structure. Is it arranged in the best possible way?

• Content. Do you need to include more details or background information? Are any topics not covered that should be? Can you cut anything?

Every writer has his or her own way of tackling revisions. With practice, you will find a method that suits you. Here are some tips to help you get started.

1. Between drafts, let your writing sit overnight or longer if you have time. You will come back to it the next day with fresh eyes.

2. Read through your writing once from beginning to end to get a general impression before you start picking away at individual sections. Write your general impressions in the margins as you go.

3. After you have read through your draft and made some changes, show your work to other people: preferably members of your intended audience. Ask them for a general impression, but be sure to give them some specific questions as well, based on the problems you have already tried to correct.

4. If you are working on a computer, take time to print out a hard copy of each draft. If you are writing by hand, recopy your work often. It will look much better on a clean, fresh page.

5. Revise and rewrite as often as you feel is necessary or have time for. Use the checklist provided on the next page to be sure you have covered all the important points.

6. The line between revising and editing is blurry. Feel free to make stylistic or grammatical changes as you revise, but try not to get caught up in editorial details when you are still trying to get the whole work properly organized and focused.

Revising Structure

1. Create an outline or tree diagram based on the way your draft is organized.

2. Reorganize the outline until you are satisfied, then rewrite the draft following the new outline.

Revising Content

1. Use your new outline to evaluate the content. Are all your main ideas well supported? If not, consider adding more support, including the information in another section, or cutting the idea altogether.

2. Ask yourself questions about the topic. Have you anticipated the questions your audience will have?

3. Is any information irrelevant? Go through each paragraph and decide whether your writing would still work if any information was removed. If the answer is yes, cut it.

Revising Focus

Finally, read over your work again, and answer the following questions:

- Have I accomplished my purpose?
- Have I addressed my audience's concerns?
- Have I taken into account the audience's degree of knowledge, expectations, and interests?

If you are still unsatisfied with any of these three areas, go back over your content and organization. Remember that most good authors revise their first draft many times. In fact, the more you revise, the better your work will likely be.

F I N A L   R E V I S I N G   C H E C K L I S T

Have I:

- ☑ Fulfilled my purpose?
- ☑ Considered my audience?
- ☑ Presented my ideas in a logical order?
- ☑ Made it easy for my readers to follow my train of thought?
- ☑ Backed up each main idea with supporting ideas and details?
- ☑ Checked that my facts are accurate?
- ☑ Included all the information my audience needs?
- ☑ Cut any material that was not essential?

WRITING GROUPS

A writing group can be very useful throughout the writing process, especially at the revising and editing stages. Chapter 7 has advice on how to make groups work smoothly. To make your writing group effective, try to meet regularly and keep the size of the group to no more than five or six people. As an author, don't get defensive, and make sure you understand the criticisms raised. Use your own judgment in deciding whether to accept a suggested revision. As a reader, make sure your criticism is honest, constructive, and specific. You can use a checklist like this one for evaluating pieces of writing.

WRITING GROUP CHECKLIST

Focus:

☑ What do you think the author was trying to accomplish?

Structure:

☑ Are the paragraphs well structured and logically linked?

☑ Is the train of thought easy to follow?

☑ Is the topic introduced clearly?

☑ If it is a thesis essay, is the thesis well worded?

☑ Does the conclusion sum up everything without being boring and repetitive? Does it mention all the main points?

List your general comments on structure.

Style:

☑ Is it enjoyable to read?

☑ Does the writing flow?

☑ Does the writer use specific vocabulary and vivid words?

☑ Is there a logical connection between ideas?

☑ Are connecting words (such as *thus, however, but, furthermore*) used properly?

☑ Is the tone appropriate?

List any other comments on style.

Content:

☑ Was there enough information?

☑ Was there too much information?

☑ Were lots of examples given?

☑ Do the examples given really prove the points, or do they seem to be just filler?

☑ Is the amount of quotation used suitable?

☑ Are quotations introduced sufficiently?

☑ Did the author answer your questions?

List your comments on content.

Overall Impression:

List at least one positive feature and at least one area that needs improvement.

EDITING

Once you have rewritten your first draft to the point where you are happy with its content, focus, and organization, look for ways to improve your writing style. Style has to do with how you write, rather than what you have to say.

EDIT YOUR DRAFT

One approach to improving your writing is to focus first on paragraphs, then on sentences, and finally on words and phrases. Use the checklists provided in this chapter to make sure you have covered each adequately.

> Feel free to develop your own method of editing your work. However, it is a good idea to use a checklist at the end of the editing process to make sure you have covered important points.

1. Go through your paper at least once to improve your paragraphs. Use the guidelines and checklist provided in this chapter to focus your editing.

2. When you are satisfied with your paragraphs, move on to individual sentences. Again, use the guidelines and checklist provided later in this chapter.

3. Then, read through the draft looking for ways to refine your word choices, using the guidelines and checklist provided here.

4. After you have worked through the checklists for paragraphs, sentences, and words and phrases, go through the final editing checklist at the end of the chapter.

5. Use editing symbols to edit your work on paper. If you are working on computer, be sure to save a copy of your draft before you begin to edit and as you finish each of the three editing stages.

6. Be ruthless. Cut all unnecessary or inappropriate material.

7. Remember your audience and purpose when you are editing. They will affect everything from the length of your paragraphs, to the types of sentences you use, to your choice of words.

8. Concentrate more on how you write than on the content, but feel free to cycle back to the revising stage at any time if you think a change is needed.

9. Get someone you trust to look over your work after you have edited it.

> If you use a computer grammar checker, weigh every suggested change carefully, and don't consider it a substitute for a careful edit. For example, many grammar checkers will suggest replacing every single example of passive voice. It is good to avoid using the passive voice, but there are times when it makes sense. Review the rules, and make your own decision.

Here is part of an edited draft of an essay. You will find the final version in Chapter 4. The editing marks that are used on the draft are explained in the following chart. These marks are a useful shorthand to use when revising your draft because your corrections will show up clearly.

EDITING MARKS		
∧	-insert a letter or word	I passed the exam. *history* I passed the hist*o*ry exam.
ℓ	- delete a letter or word	I passed ~~the~~ my exam. I fin~~n~~ished early.
¶	- begin a new paragraph	¶The physics exam is tomorrow.
≡	- change to a capital letter	canada
/	- change to lower case	Physics
∼	- transpose	She a*k*sed what should we study.
⊙	- insert a period	The movie was too long⊙
∧	- insert a comma	I ate popcorn, licorice, and chips.
∨	- insert an apostrophe	The theatres seats are uncomfortable.
#	- insert a space	I almost fell asleep.
....	- leave it as is	I hope ~~never~~ to go there again.

Cloning Express

At the American Fertility Society in Montreal, Jerry Hall reported an extraordinary new experiment in October 1993. He had accomplished something that ~~people~~ *science fiction fanatics* only ever dreamed about. Using a ~~new~~ *n innovative* technique, Hall cloned ~~seventeen~~ *17* human embryos into 48. The technique*?* ~~was~~ *He* wait*ed* ~~ing~~ for the embryo to divide into two, then he stripped the outer coating to sep*a*rate the *two* ~~2~~ cells, and *finally* replaced ~~finally~~ the outer coating with an artificial one. Two embryos with the exact same genetic information were manufactured. Essentially, they were two of the exact same human being. Two humans which could be made into four *Or* eight *Or* sixteen. The very idea that this could be done is overwhelming—even fascinating. It's tempting to imagine all of the possibilities that Hall's experiment exposes, *But* ~~however~~ like a dark cloud looming over a parade, *one thing* ~~the fact~~ remains ~~that~~ cloning human embryos is completely mora*ll*y wrong.

Hall had ~~He was~~ us*ed* ~~ing~~ a defective embryo to begin his experiment in order that the replicated embryos would ultimately be destroyed *by nature*. Although the embryos died by natural causes and not by an outside force, the experiment is not justified by any means ~~at all~~. The fact remains that the possibility of cloning is *now open* ~~possible~~. It is horrifying ~~and terrible to try~~ to think of the ways in which clones could be used. Parents could produce extra embryos of their child to insure that they would have access to perfectly compatible spare parts from the clones for a child who might need it in the future. Or worse yet, clones could be produced for parts, to be sold commercially ~~in order to make money~~. A couple could find their ideal child, both physically and *in personality* ~~mentally,~~ and buy a cloned embryo to raise that exact child.

Writing Solid Paragraphs   A paragraph is a unit of information. It is also one of the basic units of writing, along with sentences and words. Here are some characteristics of good paragraphs.

1. Focus. Each paragraph should centre on one main idea that is related to the subject of the whole piece. The main idea is often stated in one sentence in the paragraph, called a topic sentence. Topic sentences aren't used in fiction, and they are not always appropriate in non-fiction. They are most useful in expository and persuasive writing. However, remember that *all* paragraphs should express one main idea.

2. Structure. Arrange the sentences within a paragraph in a logical order, using a method of development that suits the main idea of the sentence, and make sure there is a logical flow of ideas from one sentence to the next.

However, the arrangement of a particular paragraph does not have to match the way you have chosen to arrange the work as a whole. Your history essay may be arranged by order of importance, but it could contain a particular paragraph describing a relevant event that is presented chronologically.

3. Flow. As well as being relevant to the topic of the whole piece, each paragraph should be linked clearly and logically to those before and after it.

CHECKLIST FOR EDITING PARAGRAPHS

Issue	Tips and Techniques	Help!
☑ Is each paragraph focused on one main idea?	Give each paragraph a heading or title (in your head, not in your writing). If you cannot think of a title, consider rewriting it with a clearer focus. Cut any unnecessary or repetitive sentences.	
☑ Is each paragraph arranged logically?	Use the methods of arrangement described in Chapter 1 to structure the sentences in your paragraph.	Organize Your Thoughts, page 13
☑ Does each paragraph flow into the one before and the one after?	Read the last line of the first paragraph and the first line of the following paragraph. Is a transitional word or phrase needed?	Transitions, page 31
☑ Does each sentence within a paragraph flow logically into the one before and the one after?		Transitions, page 31

Writing Interesting Sentences

A sentence is a group of words that expresses a complete thought. Every sentence contains a verb and a subject (stated or implied). If you want your writing to sound polished, you need to write sentences that interest your reader. When you edit, aim to develop the following aspects of your sentences.

1. Clarity. Write sentences that are complete and correct. Each sentence should express a complete thought. Each should also have a stated or implied subject as well as a verb, and the subject and the verb should agree.

2. Simplicity. Avoid trying to say too much in one sentence, and arrange the phrases and clauses within a sentence to avoid ambiguity. If there is a simpler way to say something, do so. Cut unnecessary words and phrases heartlessly!

3. Rhythm. Write some short and some long sentences, and use different constructions to create rhythm and emphasis in your writing.

> Variety is important, but don't sacrifice simplicity or clarity. It is easier to add some variety after the fact to simple, straightforward writing than it is to rewrite complicated, artificial prose to make it clear.

CHECKLIST FOR EDITING SENTENCES

Issue	Tips and Techniques	Help!
✔ Does your writing flow?	Read each paragraph aloud and listen for the rhythm of the sentences. Note areas that are pleasing to listen to. Vary your sentence structure to smooth over areas that are too jarring.	Sentence Variety, page 34
✔ Are important statements emphasized?	Use one or two short, simple sentences to draw attention to a particular sentence.	Sentence Variety, page 34
	Arrange phrases and clauses logically within the sentence to avoid ambiguity and to emphasize the main idea.	Awkward Sentences, page 38 Word Order and Ideas, page 46
✔ Is the tone of each sentence appropriate to your purpose and audience?	Look for sudden lapses in the level of formality, inappropriate sarcasm or emotion, or any other change in tone that does not fit.	Tone, page 17 Formality, page 19 Tone and Sentence Type, page 46

☑ Is each sentence clear?	Don't try to say too much in a single sentence.	Awkward Sentences, page 38
	Use the active voice whenever possible.	Active and Passive Voice, page 44
	Check carefully for misplaced or dangling modifiers and faulty parallelism.	Modifier Mistakes, page 37
		Parallelism, page 40
☑ Is each sentence correct?	Read backwards, from the last sentence to the first, to check for sentence fragments.	Sentence Fragments, page 35
	Correct run-on sentences.	Run-on Sentences, page 37
	Make sure verbs agree with their subjects, especially in sentences that contain indefinite pronouns.	Subject-Verb Agreement, page 40
	Avoid gender bias in your use of pronouns.	Gender Bias, page 42

STYLE, GRAMMAR, AND USAGE

Your choice of words can have a startling impact on your writing. Choose words that are precise, appropriate, and powerful. Here are some tips to help you hone your writing skill.

1. *Precision.* Replace general, vague words or expressions with more specific ones. Omit unnecessary or redundant words. In general, try to find ways to reduce the number of words you need to convey your message.

2. *Propriety.* Use language that is appropriate to your audience, purpose, and the degree of formality of your work. For example, avoid using colloquial expressions in formal writing, and use less complicated vocabulary when you are writing for a younger audience. Explain or replace words that your audience may not understand.

3. *Power.* The fresher and more direct your words are, the more impressive your writing will be. Avoid overused clichés and figures of speech and choose individual words that create a strong impression. A dictionary or thesaurus will help you find the replacements.

CHECKLIST FOR EDITING WORDS AND PHRASES

Issue	Tips and Techniques	Help!
☑ Have I chosen specific words rather than vague, general terms?	Whenever possible, replace nouns or verbs accompanied by modifiers (adjectives and adverbs) with a single, more precise noun or verb (instead of "female horse," say "mare").	
	Replace forms of the verb "be" with more interesting and precise verbs.	
	Watch out for pronouns without clear antecedents.	Precise Pronouns, page 46
	Use euphemisms only when they suit your purpose and audience.	Euphemisms, page 56
☑ Have I used correct words and expressions?	Check out the list of commonly confused words in this chapter, and start a list of your own.	Commonly Confused Words, page 51
	Use the right pronoun case.	Precise Pronouns, page 46
	Avoid mixed metaphors.	Figures of Speech, page 55
☑ Have I cut all unnecessary words and phrases?	Omit all redundant words or expressions.	Redundancy, page 49
	Avoid double negatives.	Double Negatives, page 51
☑ Have I created fresh, striking sounds and images?	Avoid overused or obscure words and expressions.	Clichés, page 55 Jargon, page 56 Affected Language, page 56
	Use Alliteration for emphasis (sparingly in non-fiction). Avoid repeating the same word too often.	Alliteration, page 57 Repetition, page 50

Transitions   Creating links between sentences and between clauses within the same sentence will help your reader to follow your train of thought and make your writing more coherent. Here are four ways to make transitions.

1. Use a pronoun to refer to a person or idea just mentioned.

Weak: Victoria Beach, Manitoba is a great place to spend a summer. The six beaches are all good for swimming.

Strong: Victoria Beach, Manitoba is a great place to spend a summer. *Its* six beaches are all good for swimming.

2. Repeat a key word.

Weak: After the Second World War, Germany was divided into two separate countries by the Berlin Wall. For many, destroying it symbolized the end of the Cold War.

Strong: After the Second World War, Germany was divided into two separate countries by the Berlin Wall. For many, destroying *the Wall* symbolized the end of the Cold War.

3. Refer directly to the preceding idea using a synonym.

Weak: Several species of rattlesnakes are native to Canada. Rocky outcrops are a favourite hangout.

Strong: Several species of rattlesnakes are native to Canada. Rocky outcrops are a favourite hangout *for these vipers*.

4. Use a transitional expression.

Weak: I'd love to go out with you tonight. I have a slight dose of the flu.

Strong: I'd love to go out with you tonight, *but* I have a slight dose of the flu.

Here is a list of some common transitional expressions, arranged by category.

Cause and Effect	Summary	Explanation
accordingly	from what has been said	for example
as a result	in brief	for instance
because	in conclusion	incidentally
consequently	in general	indeed
since	in short	in fact
therefore	in summary	in other words
thus		in particular
		namely
		specifically
		that is

Comparison	Place	Purpose
by way of comparison	beside	for this purpose
compare	beyond	for this reason
in a similar way	here	to this end
likewise	on the other side	with this in mind
similarly	opposite	
	there	

Addition	Time	Contrast
additionally	after a while	although
again	afterwards	at the same time
also, too	at last	but
at the same time	at length	even though
besides	eventually	however
equally important	finally	in contrast
finally	immediately	in spite of
further	in the future	instead
furthermore	in the past	nevertheless
in addition	meanwhile	on the contrary
lastly	soon	still
moreover	subsequently	though
next	ultimately	

> Only use transitions to link thoughts that are related, and do not overuse any one type of transition in a single assignment.

T R Y I T !

▶ *Rewrite each of the following sets of sentences to improve their clarity. Use one of the methods described in this chapter.*

Care for a crisp, juicy grasshopper for breakfast? In many parts of the world, it is considered perfectly acceptable to eat.

North American culture is revolted by the thought of eating bugs. Locusts, grasshoppers, ants, and bees are considered delicacies by some people.

Even stinkbugs are eaten and enjoyed in some parts of the world. The glands contain cyanide, which is poisonous.

Why do some societies eat insects? For one thing, they are an abundant protein source. Areas like the rainforest do not have many, since there is no room to plant crops and large animals are hard to come by.

The real question is not "Why do some people eat insects?" Why does our culture not think of insects as food? We gladly devour crab and lobster, in spite of their insect-like appearance. Why do we consider them taboo?

Sentence Variety

SENTENCE TYPE	EXAMPLES	DEFINITION
simple	The cow mooed. The chicken saw the axe. The donkey and the walrus ran off together. The farmer howled and brayed.	A group of related words that express a single thought, and which comprise a single subject and a single predicate (verb). Note, however, that either the subject or the verb (or both) may be compound.
compound	The end of the world is nigh, and I don't have a thing to wear. Jared stared, but then he shook his head in disbelief.	Two simple sentences joined by a comma and a coordinating conjunction (*and, or, nor, for, but, so, yet*). Note that each simple sentence within the compound must have its own subject.
complex	After the donkey and the walrus ran off together, the farmer howled and brayed. Jared stared when the cow mooed.	Two simple sentences joined together by a subordinating conjunction (see the list under *Transitions*, on page 31).

The table above shows three types of sentence structure: simple, compound, and complex. If you use too many simple sentences, your writing will sound choppy. On the other hand, too many compound or complex sentences can sound long and monotonous. Listen to how your writing sounds, and add variety to awkward sections by combining parts of sentences or whole sentences.

> Try reading your work out loud to a friend or your writing group, or into a tape recorder. Ask your audience to listen for choppy sounding parts and for sections that are too slow-moving.

Use coordinating and subordinating conjunctions to transform simple sentences into compound or complex sentences.

The moose flirted. I fled.
The moose flirted, *but* I fled.
When the moose flirted, I fled.

The dog rolled over. He played dead.
The dog rolled over *and* played dead.
After the dog rolled over, he played dead.

Yesterday dragged on forever. Today has dragged on forever too.
Yesterday *and* today have dragged on forever.
Yesterday dragged on forever *and so* has today.

Coordinating Conjunctions

and	for	yet
or	but	
nor	so	

Subordinating Conjunctions

after	even if	though
although	even though	unless
as	if	until
as if	in order that	when
as long as	provided that	whenever
as much as	since	where
as soon as	so that	wherever
because	than	whether
before	that	while

T R Y I T !

▶ *Rewrite the following passage to improve the rhythm and sentence variety.*

The Jim twins are twin brothers. They were separated at birth. Both boys were adopted into different families. Both were named James by their adoptive parents. They were reunited at the age of thirty-nine. Then a string of astonishing similarities was discovered in their lives. Both had been married to women named Linda. They remarried women named Betty. Jim Springer had a son named James Allan. He had an adopted brother named Larry. His twin brother, Jim Lewis, had a son named James Alan. He had an adopted brother named Larry, too. Each brother named a pet dog Toy. Both brothers had been part-time deputy sheriffs in the state of Ohio. Both had driven a Chevrolet from Ohio to the same place in Florida. The place was only three blocks long. Both brothers are six feet tall. Both brothers weigh 180 pounds. Both suffer from tension headaches. The headaches started when they were 18 years old. Both did mechanical drawing. They both used block lettering. Each brother liked carpentry.

Sentence Fragments

A fragment is a part of a sentence, punctuated as if the words form a complete sentence. Sentence fragments are sometimes acceptable in informal writing, in dialogue, or in fiction. Do not use them in formal writing, though.

Avoid: According to W.W. Rostow, countries develop in five stages. *From traditional societies to the stage of high mass consumption.* (no verb or subject in the second sentence)

Acceptable: According to W.W. Rostow, countries develop in five stages, from traditional societies to the stage of high mass consumption.

Avoid: Why do people pay money to get scared out of their wits? *For example, roller coasters, horror movies, and skydiving.* (no verb or subject in second sentence)

Acceptable: Why do people pay money to get scared out of their wits? Why, for example, do we ride roller coasters, go to horror movies, or try skydiving?

Avoid: Try tree planting in Northern British Columbia. *If you aren't afraid of hard work.* (incomplete thought in second sentence needs to be attached to another clause)

Acceptable: If you aren't afraid of hard work, try tree planting in Northern British Columbia.

These examples show there are many ways to fix sentence fragments. You can add words to the fragment to make a complete sentence, or you can change the punctuation so the fragment forms part of the previous sentence.

Fragments often finish a thought started in a previous sentence. Try reading back to front, starting from the last sentence in your writing and working back to the beginning. As you read each sentence on its own, make sure each has its own subject and verb and ask yourself whether it expresses a complete thought.

TRY IT!

1. Identify the sentence fragments in the following passage.

Picnics are no fun. Bugs, dirt, poison ivy. Eating soggy sandwiches. The strawberries squashed at the bottom of the basket. Wouldn't you really prefer a civilized meal in a civilized restaurant, where all the cooking is done for you? No dishes to clean, no pots to scrub. Bugs rarely in evidence. You can always open a window to get a dose of fresh air. If you *want* fresh air. I prefer air conditioning. So. Next time someone suggests a picnic, take my advice. Run!

2. Now rewrite the passage to make it sound more formal by eliminating the sentence fragments you identified.

Run-on Sentences

CROSS-REFERENCE

▶ Coordinating and subordinating conjunctions are listed on page 35.

A run-on sentence is made up of two or more complete thoughts that are joined together by only a comma, or simply written as one sentence with no punctuation at all.

You *can* have two complete thoughts in a single sentence. Such a sentence is called a compound sentence. However, you need to join the two thoughts together using either a coordinating conjunction (*and, or, nor, for, but, so,* or *yet*) or a subordinating conjunction (*because, if, when, as, although, whether,* etc.).

Avoid: That man is very wealthy, he owns a hair replacement clinic.

Acceptable: That man is very wealthy. He owns a hair replacement clinic.

Avoid: We went to Niagara Falls for the day, we enjoyed the mini-golf and wax museums, the Falls were closed for repair.

Acceptable: We went to Niagara Falls for the day. We enjoyed the mini-golf and wax museums, but the Falls were closed for repair.

TRY IT!

▶ *Rewrite the following paragraph, eliminating any run-on sentences.* Alberta singer k.d. lang caused quite a furor when she appeared in a commercial proclaiming that "meat stinks," she offended a lot of people in the province who depend on cattle for their livelihood. Some animal rights activists would agree with lang, they feel that killing animals for food is immoral. Others believe that although we must protect animals from cruel treatment, it is all right to eat meat. These same moderates also tend to believe that using animals in research is sometimes justified however the hard-liners oppose any such use. Some radical activists have turned to violence to make their point, bombing meat markets and breaking into labs to free animals.

Modifier Mistakes

A modifier is a word or phrase that describes another word or phrase in a sentence. There are two common mistakes writers make with modifiers: misplacing them and dangling them.

MISPLACED MODIFIERS

Keep modifiers close to the word they describe. Here are some examples of misplaced modifiers. The arrows show how to correct the sentences.

Elise sat waiting for her boyfriend to arrive *in a black silk dress*.

It hurt so much that I screamed *almost*.

Our apartment was finished *barely* when we first moved in.

DANGLING MODIFIERS

A dangling modifier is a descriptive word or phrase that does not refer to anything in the sentence. It confuses the reader.

Avoid: Sailing over the outfield wall, the crowd went wild.

Acceptable: As the ball went sailing over the outfield wall, the crowd went wild.

Avoid: Instead of hanging on the hook, I left my keys in the car.

Acceptable: Instead of hanging them on the hook, I left my keys in the car.

Avoid: Full of hot air, the man stood in the basket of the balloon.

Acceptable: The man stood in the basket of the balloon full of hot air.

Acceptable: The man stood in the basket of the hot-air balloon.

T R Y I T !

▶ *Rewrite this paragraph, eliminating any dangling or misplaced modifiers by rearranging parts of the sentence, or rewording.*

On December 6, 1917, two ships collided in Halifax Harbour called the *Mont Blanc* and the *Imo*. The *Mont Blanc's* cargo of highly explosive materials caught fire and drifted in toward Halifax's north shore, including picric acid, TNT, and benzene. At 9:06 a.m., the ship blew up, producing the largest artificial explosion the world has ever seen, except for the bombing of Hiroshima. Disintegrating into a shower of metal fragments, the destruction caused by the vessel was horrific. Hurled five-and-a-half kilometres, rescue crews found a gun from the *Mont Blanc* embedded in the ground at Armbro Lake. All houses were either flattened by the blast or burned in the north end of the city. Out of a total population of 50 000 people, 9600, or one-fifth, were killed or injured almost. Twenty thousand people in the middle of a blizzard were left with inadequate shelter and 6000 were completely left homeless for several days after the explosion.

Awkward Sentences

There are many kinds of awkward sentences. Here are some suggestions to help you simplify awkward sentences.

- Isolate the main thought in the sentence from the secondary, less important thoughts.

Avoid: In the end, after many battles, and not before they had exhausted all legal avenues open to them, with their heads held high, they gave up the fight.

Acceptable: In the end, they gave up the fight, but with their heads held high and not before they had exhausted all legal avenues open to them.

- Keep subjects and verbs as close together as possible.

Avoid: This summer, Juan and I, whether we are working or not, will spend a lot of time together.

Acceptable: Juan and I will spend a lot of time together this summer, whether we are working or not.

- Place modifiers close to the word they modify.

Avoid: In 1987, representatives from 24 countries agreed, gradually, over ten years, including Canada, to reduce their CFC use.

Acceptable: In 1987, representatives from 24 countries including Canada agreed to reduce their CFC use gradually over ten years.

- Don't try to pack too much information into a single sentence.

Avoid: Intercropping, which involves planting mixed crops in the same field and changing the types of crops every year, and which is a common practice in many developing countries, because planting one crop over and over again can deplete the soil of specific nutrients, which allows bugs to attack the plants, is an important part of pest control.

Acceptable: Intercropping, which involves planting mixed crops in the same field and changing the types of crops every year, is a common practice in many developing countries. This agricultural method is an important part of pest control, because planting one crop over and over again can deplete the soil of specific nutrients.

TRY IT!

▶ *Rewrite the following passage simplifying any awkward sentences.*

Hippocrates, a Greek philosopher who lived in the fifth century, as a way of explaining temperament, developed the theory of the four humours, or fluids, namely blood, yellow bile, black bile, and phlegm. When an individual tended to be sanguine, or excitable, he or she had, according to Hippocrates, an excess of blood, or *sanguis*. Similarly, too much yellow bile made one quick to anger, while black bile produced melancholy, and phlegm tended to make one slow and apathetic. Although for many years modern researchers dismissed Hippocrates' theory, along with all theories of personality that claim nature or biology as a major influence, and claimed that, in fact, nurture was a much greater factor in determining personality, some are now re-examining the idea that we are born with at least a tendency to a particular temperament, and are proposing personality types linked to the level of naturally occurring hormones in the body. For example, instead of brave, outgoing individuals, as Hippocrates believed, having an excess of blood, some scientists have discovered that these individuals have high levels of serotonin in their bodies, while those who tend to be quick to anger, whom the ancients would have called "choleric," or having an excess of yellow bile, have much lower levels of this hormone.

Parallelism

The clearest way to list similar items or events in a series is to make them match one another in form. Expressing corresponding elements in the same grammatical form is called *parallelism*. All items in a series should be in parallel form—all nouns, all prepositional phrases, all adverb clauses, and so on. Parallel structure makes the series clear and easy to follow. Items in a list should also be parallel in structure.

Avoid: When I babysit, I like baring my teeth, rolling my eyes, and to stick my tongue out to scare the little tykes. (three verbs in series are not parallel in form)

Acceptable: When I babysit, I like baring my teeth, rolling my eyes, and sticking my tongue out to scare the little tykes.

Avoid: Self-possession, being agile, and a sense of humour are all useful when dealing with young children. (only two of the three items in series are nouns)

Acceptable: Self-possession, agility, and a sense of humour are all useful when dealing with young children.

TRY IT!

▶ *Rewrite the following passage, changing words, phrases, or sentences as necessary to avoid faulty parallels.*

I once babysat for a real troublemaker: a three-year-old boy with blond hair, an angelic smile, and used to getting his own way. As soon as his parents left, he would cry, scream, and threw himself on the couch. The only way to calm him down was to give him food, read him a story, or letting him watch TV. Once he disappeared while he was supposed to be watching cartoons. I called his name, ran all over the house, unable to find him. At last he sauntered into the living room calmly, with an innocent look, and triumphantly, just as I was picking up the phone to call the police. He never told me where he had been; I never told his parents he was missing; and they never did understand why from then on I was always busy when they asked me to babysit!

Subject-Verb Agreement

Every sentence has a subject (stated or implied) and a verb. A singular subject takes a singular verb; a plural subject takes a plural verb. Usually, you will have no problem deciding what form of verb to use in a sentence. Whenever you are in doubt, check over the following list of special situations.

PLURAL-SOUNDING ENDINGS

Some nouns sound as if they are plural because they end in -s, but they are actually singular. Some examples are *news, mumps, measles, physics, mathematics,* and *economics.*

The *news is* not good: *measles is* still the cause of millions of deaths among young children in poor countries.

COMPOUND SUBJECTS

When the subject of the sentence is made up of two or more singular nouns joined together by the word *and*, use a plural verb.

Her *mittens, scarf, and ears were* a beautiful shade of blue on that cold morning.

EITHER...OR AND SIMILAR WORD PAIRS

When a compound subject is linked by words such as *either...or, neither...nor, not only...but also*, and *whether...or*, make the verb agree with the part of the subject that is closest to the verb.

Not only my wallet but also my *false teeth were* stolen.

Neither the teeth nor the *wallet was* ever found.

Compound subjects joined by *or* or *nor* usually sound better if the plural part of the subject is placed closest to the verb.

COLLECTIVE NOUNS

Nouns that name a group of people or things, such as *group, army, crowd, bunch,* and *family*, usually take a singular verb.

A *bunch* of grapes *was* glued to her hat.

INDEFINITE PRONOUNS

Indefinite pronouns ending in -one, -body, and -thing always require a singular verb. Here is a list of some of these pronouns:

Everyone loves my pet ferret.

Nobody knows the trouble I've seen.

Something is better than nothing.

The indefinite pronouns *some, more, all, none, most,* and *any* can be either singular or plural, depending on their use in a specific sentence.

All of the apple pie *is* gone.

All of the apple pies *are* gone.

T R Y I T !

▶ *Choose the correct word from each pair inside the square brackets.*

Mathematics [is / are] a lot easier when you have a computer or calculator in front of you. But not everyone [needs / need] this kind of help; mathematical prodigies turn up every so often who can mentally calculate sums that even electronic instruments [find / finds] challenging. Some of them [claim / claims] to see the numbers, while other prodigies associate numbers with sounds; furthermore, most [calculate / calculates] from left to right, rather than right to left as we are usually taught. One of the greatest among recent prodigies [is / are] a woman called Shakuntala Devi, who has toured the world demonstrating her remarkable ability. (Unfortunately, neither your pocket calculators nor Ms. Devi [is / are] allowed at your desk during the math exam.)

Gender Bias

Avoid using sexist language of any kind in your writing. Here are some common examples of gender bias to watch out for.

Avoid: The two mayoral candidates appeared in an all-candidates meeting last night. Ms. Karkov, a petite blonde, wore a yellow blouse and black skirt and pledged to encourage more industries to locate in the area. Mr. Dressler spoke impressively about his commitment to better housing within the city.

Acceptable: The two mayoral candidates appeared in an all-candidates meeting last night. Ms. Karkov pledged to encourage more industries to locate in the area. Mr. Dressler spoke impressively about his commitment to better housing within the city.

It is not necessarily bad to describe the way people look or what they are wearing. Doing so can add colour and interest to your writing. Just be sure that the characteristics and details you describe are relevant to your purpose, and that they are not presented as stereotypes.

Avoid: Mr. and Mrs. Paul Desrosiers arrived in a black limousine.

Acceptable: Mr. Paul Desrosiers and his wife, Ms. Céline Laplante-Desrosiers, arrived in a black limousine.

Avoid: Mr. Delvecchio, meet Mr. Hamid, Mr. Dawson, and Sophie, our secretary.

Acceptable: Santo Delvecchio, meet David Hamid and Stuart Dawson, who are heading up the production team, and Sophie Sourtsis, our secretary.

Acceptable: Mr. Delvecchio, meet Mr. Hamid, Mr. Dawson, and Ms. Sourtsis.

SEXIST WORDS

Here is a list of words that you should avoid in your writing, along with some suggested replacements.

WORDS TO AVOID	SUGGESTED REPLACEMENTS
businessman	executive, businessperson, entrepreneur, manager
chairman	chairperson, chair
housewife	homemaker
mailman	letter carrier, postal worker
man, mankind	humanity, human beings, humankind, people, the human race
poetess	poet
policeman	police officer
salesman	salesperson, sales clerk, sales attendant
stewardess	flight attendant
waitress	server, attendant
workman	worker, employe

PRONOUNS AND GENDER

In English, we do not have a personal pronoun (like *he* or *she*) that covers both sexes. This can be a problem when a personal pronoun refers back to an indefinite singular pronoun or when the sex of the person is irrelevant.

Avoid: Whoever parked *their* bike against the telephone pole is in for an unpleasant surprise: only the lock is left!

Acceptable: Whoever parked *his or her* bike against the telephone pole is in for an unpleasant surprise: only the lock is left!

> It is all right to use *their* to replace *his or her* in casual spoken English. However, it is still not acceptable in formal writing.

Too many *his or her's* can be cumbersome. Here are some other ways to get around the issue of gender in pronouns.

- In longer pieces of writing, alternate using male and female personal pronouns. That is, use she (or her) in one instance and he (or him) the next time the problem arises. Be sure not to alternate genders within the same example.

Avoid: If a teenager is treated fairly by *her* parents, *he* will respond reasonably.

Acceptable: If a teenager is treated fairly by *her* parents, *she* will respond reasonably.

• Change the sentence from singular to plural.

Avoid: In Japan, a visitor should leave his shoes at the door before entering a house.

Acceptable: In Japan, visitors should leave their shoes at the door before entering a house.

• Replace the pronoun with *you* or *one*.

Avoid: When a client uses a debit card to pay for his purchases, he simply punches his PIN number into a machine, and the money is automatically deducted from his bank account.

Acceptable: When one uses a debit card to pay for one's purchases, one simply punches a PIN number into a machine, and the money is automatically deducted from one's bank account.

Acceptable: When you use a debit card to pay for your purchases, simply punch your PIN number into a machine, and the money is automatically deducted from your bank account.

> Use *one* only in formal writing, and use it sparingly. It tends to sound stilted and old fashioned if it is overused. *You* is more friendly and usually works just as well.

• Reword the sentence so you do not need a personal pronoun.

Avoid: A true birdwatcher never forgets his binoculars.

Acceptable: A true birdwatcher is never without binoculars.

A P P L Y   I T !

▶ *Gender bias is sometimes still present in the media. Look for an example of sexist language in local newspapers or magazines and write a letter about it to the editors.*

Active and Passive Voice

Usually, the subject of the verb performs the action named in the verb. When this is the case, the verb is in the *active voice*. For example:

Jaffra sniffed the pepper. (Who sniffed? Jaffra did.)

Josh thought about lawn chairs. (Who thought? Josh did.)

Mariko cuffed the criminal. (Who cuffed? Mariko did.)

However, in the following sentences, the subject of the sentence is not the one who performs the action.

My wallet has been stolen! (The wallet didn't steal, a thief did.)

The baby was found on the steps of the church. (The baby did not find, someone else did.)

I was taught by my mother never to drink milk and laugh at the same time. (I didn't teach, my mother did.)

These three sentences are all in the passive voice. Use the passive voice in the following situations:

• When you do not know who performed the action.

• When the person or thing that received the action is more important than the actor.

• When you do not want to reveal who performed the action.

In all other cases, it is best to use the active voice.

> It is a mistake to use the passive voice to try to sound more formal or more important. It will just make your writing sound stuffy and long-winded. Remember, say what you have to say as simply as you can.

T R Y I T !

▶ *Rewrite the following passage, changing the passive voice to the active voice whenever possible. You may have to infer who the actor is.*

Lacrosse has several claims to distinction: it may be the oldest field sport in existence; it is certainly the oldest team sport played in North America; and, in 1760, it was used by Chief Pontiac and the Ottawas as a secret weapon in a surprise attack on Fort Michilimackinac! It seems a game of *baggataway* (the original Native name for what we now call lacrosse) was organized directly outside the gates of the impenetrable garrison by Pontiac's men. The soldiers inside the fort were intrigued by the unfamiliar sport, so the gates were opened, and they stood at a distance, watching the play. At one point, the ball was shot toward the gate by one of the players and was chased by the rest of the two teams. Before the garrison soldiers were aware of what was happening, weapons were brought out of their hiding places, and the gate was stormed.

Tone and Sentence Type

There are four types of sentences: statement, exclamation, question, and command. Each type says something distinctive about the writer's point of view. Each conveys a different tone.

Notice how dramatically the sentence type changes the writer's tone in the following examples:

Statement: We should definitely adopt a rat as our school mascot. (The writer sees no room for argument.)

Exclamation: How inspiring it would be to adopt a rat as our school mascot! (The writer is thoroughly convinced, an enthusiastic supporter of the change.)

Question: Should we adopt a rat as our school mascot? (The writer may be undecided.)

Command: Help us to adopt a rat as our school mascot. (The writer is convinced and seeking the support of others.)

Word Order and Ideas

The way you choose to arrange words and phrases in your sentences will have a significant influence on the message that you convey. Note how the emphasis in the following three sentences, all about the same topic, changes according to the arrangement of the words.

Although more than 3000 Canadian soldiers died at Vimy Ridge, *they captured a key position from the Germans*, succeeding where both British and French offensives had failed.

Although Canadian soldiers succeeded in capturing a key position from the Germans at Vimy Ridge, where both British and French offensives had failed, *more than 3000 Canadians died*.

At Vimy Ridge Canadian soldiers succeeded where both British and French offensives had failed, capturing a key position from the Germans, at the cost of more than 3000 Canadian lives.

When you revise your draft, identify the main point of each sentence, and try rearranging words and phrases to change the emphasis.

A P P L Y I T !

▶ *Choose a long sentence from your own writing and play with it. Rearrange the words and phrases to create a different emphasis.*

Precise Pronouns

A pronoun is a word that stands *for* another noun or pronoun. (The Latin prefix *pro-* means *for*.) Sometimes, choosing the wrong pronoun, or using one in the wrong way, can make your writing vague or confusing. Here are some things to watch for when you use pronouns.

PRONOUN ANTECEDENTS

The word the pronoun replaces is called its *antecedent.* The antecedent is the word that comes *before* the pronoun. (*Ante* in Latin means *before*.) Be sure that your reader can tell who or what the antecedent of a pronoun is.

Avoid: Erica and Marianne went to *her* mother's house.

Acceptable: Erica went to *her* mother's house with Marianne.

Avoid: I followed the recipe to the letter, but they don't seem to make a cake.

Acceptable: I followed the recipe to the letter, but the ingredients don't seem to make a cake.

- Pay particular attention to your use of the pronoun "this." Be sure that your readers can tell exactly what it refers to.

Unclear: In the first part of the story, the narrator describes her reactions to an incident involving a drowned boy. *This* foreshadows what happens later in the story, when the narrator's own child is almost drowned.

Clear: In the first part of the story, the narrator describes her reactions to an incident involving a drowned boy. *This unfortunate incident* foreshadows what happens later in the story, when the narrator's own child is almost drowned.

WHO AND WHOM

Who and *whom* are relative pronouns that refer to people. Use *who* the same way you would use *he*, as the subject of a verb. Use *whom* the same way you would use *him*, as the object of a verb.

My uncle, *who* is no longer with us, loved to juggle chain saws.
("*He* is no longer with us," so use *who*.)

The uncle to *whom* I owe my juggling talent had a fondness for chain saws.
("I owe my juggling talent to *him*," so use *whom*.)

Whom should I ask about a juggling career?
("I should ask *him* about a juggling career," so use *whom*.)

INDEFINITE PRONOUNS

An indefinite pronoun is a pronoun that does not specify the identity of what it refers to. Some indefinite pronouns are singular, some are plural, and some can be singular or plural depending on the context.

Pronouns ending in *-one, -body*, or *-thing* (as well as the pronoun *one*) take a singular verb.

Avoid: Somebody among us *are* lying.

Acceptable: Somebody among us *is* lying.

Avoid: Somebody forgot *their* toupée.

Acceptable: Somebody forgot *his* toupée.

In spoken English, it is quite common to use *their* to replace an indefinite pronoun, since it avoids the awkwardness of not knowing whether "somebody" (or "anybody," or "someone," etc.) is male or female. Avoid using *their* when you write anything formal, though. It is still considered incorrect.

The pronouns *some, none*, and *all* can be either singular or plural, depending on the sentence.

> *All* [meaning everything] *is* clear.

> *All* the pigs *were* squealing in delight.

> *Some* [books] *are* missing.

> *Some* [of the paint] *is* flaking off.

> *None* [of the money] *was* left.

> *None* [of the coins] *were* left.

PERSONAL PRONOUNS

Here is a list of personal pronouns:

Nominative	Objective
I	me
you	you
he, she, it	him, her, it
we	us
you	you
they	them

Use the *nominative* form (or case) when the pronoun is the subject of a verb or when the subject follows a form of the verb *to be*. Use the *objective* form when the pronoun is the object of a verb or when it follows a preposition (*to, in, of, from, under, before, between, around, by, through*, etc.).

Usually, you will have no problem choosing which form of personal pronoun to use. If you are not sure, refer to the chart above for the right form. The sentences below show some of the more common mistakes people make in choosing a pronoun form and how to correct them.

Avoid: *Riswan and me* won the prize for best karaoke duet.

Acceptable: *Riswan and I* won the prize for best karaoke duet.

Avoid: There are too many mental roadblocks between *she and I.*

Acceptable: There are too many mental roadblocks between *her and me.*

Avoid: Us fast-food junkies can never resist a good greasy hamburger.

Acceptable: We fast-food junkies can never resist a good greasy hamburger.

T R Y I T !

▶ *Rewrite the following passage, choosing the appropriate pronoun or verb form from inside the square brackets and eliminating ambiguous pronoun references. If a sentence contains no pronoun problems, leave it as is.*

My crazy uncle Herbert told my sister and [I / me] about the Tichborne Affair when we were children, but [she / her] and I only found out recently that the incident really happened. Here is how the story goes:

When rich young Roger Tichborne is lost at sea in 1854, his mother [who / whom] is heartbroken, puts ads in newspapers around the world, in hopes of finding him alive. Eleven years later, lo and behold, someone from Australia [answer / answers] the ad!

The man [who / whom] appears on Lady Tichborne's doorstep, claiming to be heir to the family fortune, is not very convincing to those who know him well. Most [dismiss / dismisses] him as a fraud, but none [have / has] counted on the strength of Lady Tichborne's self-deception. Young Roger was slim, had straight dark hair, a tattoo on his right arm, and could speak French fluently, but none of these traits [appear / appears] in him. In fact, the claimant is grossly overweight, has wavy blond hair, does not have a tattoo, knows not a word of French, and speaks fondly of a grandfather [who / whom] the young Roger never met!

In spite of this, Arthur Orton almost succeeded in claiming Roger Tichborne's inheritance, thanks to the support of his doting mother. It was [she / her] who championed his cause more than anyone—although Orton did eventually manage to convince dozens of people to testify in court that he was the rightful heir. In the end, Lady Tichborne died, leaving Orton without support, and he was jailed for 14 years. Orton only confessed his deception years later when, penniless, he sold his story to a magazine for £3000.

Redundancy   Watch out for unnecessary or redundant words: when more than one word or phrase in a sentence expresses the same idea, trim the fat. For example:

Weak: In summary, I conclude that a female cow can produce more milk than a codfish can.

Acceptable: I conclude that a cow can produce more milk than a codfish.

Acceptable: In summary, a cow can produce more milk than a codfish.

Here are some redundant expressions to avoid:

INSTEAD OF...	SAY...
repeat again	repeat
true fact	fact
very unique	unique
new innovation	innovation
false lie	lie
tender one's resignation	resign
extend an invitation	invite
have a preference for	prefer
be in opposition to	oppose
give encouragement	encourage
take under consideration	consider
make an attempt	try
be in agreement	agree

Repetition Try not to repeat the same word or phrase several times in a sentence or paragraph. Find another way to express what you want to say.

> If you can't find a way to replace a repeated word by rearranging the sentence or substituting a pronoun, DON'T compromise clarity. It is better to be repetitive than to be vague.

Avoid: The light energy from the sun is absorbed by the leaves of the *plant*. The *plant's* leaves convert the light energy into chemical energy, which is stored in the plant as ATP. Meanwhile, the water taken up by the *plant's* roots reacts with the carbon dioxide in the *plant* to make glucose.

Acceptable: The light energy from the sun is absorbed by the leaves of the plant, *which* convert the light energy into chemical energy *and store it* as ATP. Meanwhile, the water taken up by *the roots* reacts with carbon dioxide to make glucose.

A P P L Y   I T !

▶ *Read through one or two of your essays, looking for examples of redundancy and repetition. Find ways to reword the examples without sacrificing the clarity of the thought.*

Double Negatives You know from math class that two negatives make a positive. When you use a negative word like *barely, scarcely, hardly*, or *never* along with the word *not*, you actually create a positive. For example:

Avoid: I am so excited I *can't barely* think!

Acceptable: I am so excited I can *barely* think!

Acceptable: I am so excited I *can't* think!

Avoid: Don't you *never* do that again!

Acceptable: Don't you *ever* do that again!

Acceptable: Never do that again!

There is no such word as *irregardless*. It is a double negative because the negative prefix *ir-* and the suffix *-less* cancel out and make a positive. The correct word is *regardless*.

Commonly Confused Words The following chart shows some common word mix-ups. These are words that look or sound alike and are often confused with one another. Start your own list and keep it in your notebook or portfolio. Whenever you come across a pair of words that you tend to mix up, add the words to your list.

WORDS	EXAMPLES	MEANINGS
accept except	The team *accepted* the trophy. Everyone *except* Malidi was at hockey practice.	verb meaning "receive" preposition meaning "but"
advice advise	Do you want my *advice*? I *advise* you to stop smoking.	noun meaning "suggestion" verb meaning "offer a suggestion"
affect effect	Nervousness *affected* my performance. Nervousness had a disastrous *effect* on my performance.	verb meaning "cause a change" noun meaning "the result of a change"
alternate alternative	They practised on *alternate* Fridays. Jean *alternated* with Jelena at centre. Since the highway was blocked, they took an *alternative* route. They had no *alternative* but to postpone the game.	adjective meaning "every other" verb meaning "take the place of" adjective meaning "other" noun meaning "other choice"

WORDS	EXAMPLES	MEANINGS
choose chose	We always *choose* our own speech topics. Last semester, I *chose* to speak on the importance of energy conservation.	verb, present tense, meaning "select" verb, past tense, meaning "selected"
coarse course	This sandpaper is *coarse*, but your jokes are *coarser*. My *course* on personal finance is held in a building right next to the race *course*. Every week, I place a bet and, of *course*, lose more money!	adjective meaning "rough, crude, not fine" has several meanings but used only as a noun or a verb
desert dessert	The frightened soldier *deserted* his companions in the *desert*. On my birthday, we had spice cake for *dessert*.	verb meaning "abandon" noun meaning "a dry region" noun meaning "sweet food served after a meal"
hear here	I think I *hear* voices. But we are the only ones *here*!	verb meaning "perceive sound through the ear" adverb meaning "in this place"
its it's	A flower turns *its* blossom toward the sun. *It's* essential for the entire plant to have light.	possessive pronoun meaning "belonging to it" contraction meaning "it is"
lead lead led	These pipes are made of *lead*. *Lead* us to the auditorium. We *led* the visitors to the auditorium.	noun meaning "a kind of metal" verb, present tense, meaning "guide" verb, past tense, meaning "guided"
loose lose	My pet python is *loose* on the streets! I hope I don't *lose* my darling snake for good.	adjective meaning "not fixed or fastened" (rhymes with *goose*) verb meaning "misplace or part with"
of 've	This is a dictionary *of* literary terms. I should*'ve* told you that.	functions only as a preposition contraction of the verb *have*
our are	How do you like *our* science display? *Are* you old enough to vote?	possessive adjective meaning "belonging to us" form of the verb "be"

WORDS	EXAMPLES	MEANINGS
passed	As the parade *passed* by, the clowns *passed* out balloons to the children in the crowd.	verb meaning "went by" or "gave"
past	In the *past*, this highway was just a dirt road. We drove *past* the dump.	noun or adjective meaning "the time before the present" adverb meaning "beyond, farther than"
principal	Ms. Montclair is the *principal* of our school.	noun meaning "chief person," adjective meaning "chief"
principle	The *principle* behind our system of law is that the accused is innocent until proven guilty.	noun meaning "a basic truth or belief"
quiet	Please be *quiet* in the library.	adjective, noun, or verb meaning "not making sound"
quite	He has not *quite* finished.	adverb meaning "completely"
quit	Please *quit* shouting at me.	verb meaning "stop"
sole	I ordered *sole* for dinner because it was the *sole* item on the menu I recognized.	noun meaning "bottom part of a shoe" or "a flat ocean fish"; adjective meaning "single" or "only"
soul	Some people believe that the *soul* lives on after the body.	noun meaning "the part of a person distinct from the body" or simply "a person"
stationary stationery	Heavy equipment is usually *stationary*. I always get *stationery* from my pen pal for Christmas.	adjective meaning "not moving" noun meaning "writing paper"
than	Mac is quicker with numbers *than* I am.	conjunction or preposition showing comparison
then	I got out my biology book, but *then* I decided I'd rather watch television than study.	adverb meaning "at that time" or "next"
their	Mammals nurse *their* young.	possessive adjective meaning "belonging to them"
there	Put your jacket over *there*.	adverb meaning "in that place"
they're	*They're* the first people in line.	contraction meaning "they are"

WORDS	EXAMPLES	MEANINGS
through	We drove *through* the Rockies on our vacation.	functions only as a preposition
threw	The catcher *threw* the ball to first.	verb, past tense, meaning "hurled" or "tossed"
to	I go *to* my skydiving lesson every Tuesday.	functions only as a preposition
too	I, *too*, ate *too* much pizza.	adverb meaning "also" and "more than enough"
two	Luigi can speak *two* languages fluently.	adjective or noun meaning "one more than one"
weather	Outdoor games are more enjoyable in fine *weather*.	noun meaning "condition of the atmosphere"
whether	She didn't know *whether* to laugh or to cry.	conjunction used to introduce a choice
were	The early settlers *were* immigrants from many countries.	past tense of "are," form of the verb "be"
where	*Where* did the settlers from France first make their homes?	adverb meaning "in what place"
which	*Which* province grows the most wheat?	functions only as a pronoun or adjective
witch	In *The Wizard of Oz*, Dorothy melts the wicked *witch* by throwing water over her.	noun meaning "woman supposed to have magical powers"
who's	*Who's* playing the part of Hamlet?	contraction meaning "who is" or "who has"
whose	I know *whose* script this is.	possessive pronoun for "who" and "which"
your	*Your* dog broke the fence.	possessive adjective meaning "belonging to you"
you're	*You're* going to have to pay for the repair of the fence.	contraction meaning "you are"

A P P L Y I T !

▶ *Rather than trying to memorize every word pair in the list above, note down the ones that give you the most trouble. Start your own list of commonly confused words, which you can add to at any time. (If you write the list on a computer, you will be able to keep it in alphabetical order.) Consult your own list every time you edit a piece of your writing.*

Figures of Speech

The most common kinds of figures of speech are similes and metaphors.

A *simile* compares one thing to another by using the word *like* or *as*.

> From the sky, an area of clear-cut forest looks like a scar.

A *metaphor* describes a thing as something else in order to suggest a likeness.

> The train winding through the valley far below is a steel snake.

- Don't use too many figures of speech in school assignments.

- When you do use similes and metaphors, make sure the image you are creating makes sense when you picture it, or you may end up with a mixed metaphor. A *mixed metaphor* is a comparison between two objects that does not make sense. Here is an example.

  > The Grand Canyon of Serena's depression reached its height when she failed her swimming test.

  The first image makes a connection between Serena's depression and the depth and vastness of the Grand Canyon. But the comparison becomes silly when the idea of height is added to the metaphor.

- Also, be sure the emotions evoked by the image are appropriate to your message. For example, the word "scar" in the simile above would evoke strong negative reactions in your readers. You wouldn't want to use such an image if you were arguing *in favour* of clear-cutting.

Cliché

A cliché is an overused expression. Most clichés began as strong images, but because they have been used so often, they have lost their ability to stir our imaginations. Avoid them like the plague! (There is an example right there.)

Here are some more clichés:

add insult to injury   in the long run

bright as a new penny
cool as a cucumber
cold as ice
easier said than done
finishing touches
good as gold

narrow escape
red-letter day
slowly but surely
this day and age
word to the wise

T R Y I T !

▶ *Rewrite one of the clichés above using a fresh new image. For example:*
   cold as metal in winter
   cool as a computer

Jargon

Jargon, in a broad sense, refers to the use of special terms or fancy phrases that hide meaning (or try to cover up a lack of meaning). Here is an example of jargon that confuses the reader:

> Positive input into the infrastructure impacts systematically on the functional base of the firm in that it stimulates a concretization of meaningful objectives from a strategic standpoint.

Chances are the writer does not have anything to say but wants to sound authoritative. When something has been written in this mixed up way, do not be intimidated; be suspicious.

Affected Language

Affected writing can be a combination of a lot of bad habits. It may be wordy, trite, redundant, awkward, or full of jargon. Some writers fall into this way of writing when they want to sound impressive. But the result is usually the opposite. The way to avoid affected language is to choose the simplest, clearest way of saying what you have to say.

Affected: Inasmuch as the Canadian mode of expression is distinct unto itself, substantially influenced though it may be by British and American usage, it would seem to be a matter of instant and obvious logic to recognize that we must maintain, in earnest, a system of orthographic conventions that is both nationalistic and appropriate to our individualistic heritage.

Unaffected: Although Canadian English has been influenced by British and American usage, Canadians should try to maintain a spelling system that is distinctly their own.

Euphemism

A euphemism is a word or phrase that names a thing in an indirect or mild way because the direct way is perceived as unpleasant or harsh.

Euphemisms can be good or bad, sensible or silly. Here are some euphemisms matched with the plain English to which they refer:

laid to rest	= buried
technical services specialist	= lab technician
developing nations	= poor countries
starter home	= small house
misleading phrase	= lie
golden age endowment	= old age pension
military solution	= war
pre-owned, reconditioned	= used
leather-like	= vinyl

Some of these euphemisms could be used for the sake of kindness or diplomacy; others are plainly designed to hide the truth. Be aware of the distinction.

Alliteration

Alliteration is using two or more words that start with the same consonant. Use alliteration in small doses to draw attention to an important word or image. For example:

Children need both *p*raise and *p*rotection.

TROUBLESHOOTING

Something is wrong, but you don't know how to fix it? Here are some suggestions.

INTEREST

Topic Seems Dull

- Change the tone: add more humour, enthusiasm, or personal anecdotes.

- Ask yourself whether you have tailored your writing to suit your audience and your purpose. Consider each paragraph in this light and cut anything that seems irrelevant or off topic.

- Link the topic to your own life and the lives of your readers.

- Use comparisons with everyday experiences and things.

- Scale things down so that your audience can relate to what you are saying. For example, in an essay on world hunger, describe a day in the life of one hungry child.

- Consider broadening or narrowing your topic.

Writing Is Dull

- Break up some of your longer sentences into short, sharp statements to emphasize particular points.

- Shorten the length of your paragraphs (but be careful to include all the relevant information and to use good transitions if you break down a longer paragraph into two shorter ones).

- If you use statistics, make them more meaningful by relating them to something familiar or by using a striking image.

Dull: Hong Kong is very crowded. It has a population density of 5400 people per square kilometre.

Relevant: Imagine if the entire population of Canada were living on Prince Edward Island and you will have an idea of how densely populated Hong Kong is.

- If your writing contains a lot of statistics, consider compiling them in a chart or graph.

- Replace forms of the verb "to be" in sentences with a more precise or more active verb.

Dull: The city of Thunder Bay is situated on Lake Superior.

Active: The city of Thunder Bay huddles along the northern shore of Lake Superior.

- Use more precise nouns (Oldsmobile instead of car; beagle instead of dog; bungalow instead of house).

- Simplify your sentences.

- Avoid clichés and overused expressions such as "sharp as a tack" or "soft as silk." Try to think of new images to replace the old ones.

- Use metaphors, descriptions, similes, and other figures of speech to appeal to your readers' senses (especially sight, hearing, smell, and touch).

CLARITY

Writing Is Confusing

- Reorganize your paragraphs using an outline or tree diagram.

- Avoid using jargon or other words your audience is not familiar with.

- Give more background information.

- Look for run-on sentences and sentence fragments.

- Use transition words to tie your paragraphs and sentences together.

- Use graphics or illustrations to make difficult points easier to understand.

Writing Lacks Focus

- Narrow your topic.

- Write a clear introduction, setting out what you intend to do.

- Link every paragraph to your introduction.

- Cut any paragraphs that seem to wander off the topic. (Try looking at each one and asking yourself if the essay would make sense without it.)

- Use specific nouns and verbs.

LANGUAGE

Too Formal

- Write in the first person ("I").

- Include an anecdote or a personal experience.

- Use contractions, such as "can't" or "won't."

- Add some humour (but make sure it is appropriate and related to the topic).

- Use occasional colloquial expressions if appropriate.

- Shorten some of your sentences, but keep a variety of lengths.

Too Informal

- Avoid using the first person ("I").

- Use conventional language only—no colloquial or slang expressions, no contractions.

- Lengthen your sentences but keep some variety, and use shorter sentences to emphasize particular points.

Writing Sounds Choppy

- Combine sentences by joining subjects, objects, verbs, phrases, or clauses.

- Avoid repeating the same words or phrases. Try using a thesaurus to find synonyms (words that mean the same thing).

LENGTH

Too Long

- Narrow your topic.

- Make an outline or tree diagram, and decide whether you could make your case without one or more of your main ideas.

- Look at each paragraph and ask yourself if it is necessary to accomplish your purpose or prove your thesis. If the writing will survive without that paragraph, cut it.

- Reduce the amount of detail in your supporting ideas.

- Look for simpler ways to say things.

Too Short

- Ask yourself whether you have accomplished your purpose. If you have, don't try to pad your writing.

- Make sure you have supported each of your ideas thoroughly.

- Add a graphic only if it is useful.

- Insert a quotation, personal anecdote, or a story that illustrates your thesis.

- As a last resort, broaden your topic to include more action, more ideas, more detail, or more arguments.

FINAL EDITING CHECKLIST

☑ Have I written solid, concise paragraphs?

☑ Is there a flow from one paragraph to the next?

☑ Do my sentences express my ideas clearly and simply?

☑ Have I varied sentence structure to create interest and flow?

☑ Are the words I have chosen precise, appropriate, and powerful?

☑ Have I checked the use of any confusing words against my own list of commonly confused words?

☑ Have I used transitions in an effective way?

☑ Have I checked all sentences for fragments, run-ons, and other mechanical errors?

►

PRESENTING YOUR WORK

*A*t last, you have reached the end of the writing process. All the challenging work of writing, revising, and editing your work is done, and all you have to do is print it out neatly and hand it in. It is tempting to skim over the presenting part of the writing process, but beware! If your reader is constantly distracted by messy handwriting and misspelled words, he or she is likely to be left with a poor image of your writing, even if your ideas are brilliant. Use this chapter to guide you through the final stages of proofreading and formatting your writing.

CONTENTS

PRESENTING WRITTEN WORK

PROOFREAD FOR SPELLING, CAPITALIZATION, AND PUNCTUATION

CROSS-REFERENCE

▶ The chart on page 11 shows how proofreading fits into the writing process.

CROSS-REFERENCE

▶ The editing symbols are on page 26.

To present a finished piece of writing, you need to

1. Proofread a final draft.

2. Format the final copy to make sure it follows all conventions and looks good on the page.

3. Make a final check.

Because you have read your work through so many times by now, it is easy to gloss over mistakes. Here are some tips to help you avoid this pitfall.

1. Always proofread your work on hard copy. Don't try to do it on a computer screen. It is too easy to miss things.

2. If possible, get a friend to proofread your work after you are through.

3. Try proofreading your work backwards, one sentence at a time. That way you will be able to concentrate on the words, rather than on the content of what you have written.

4. Make changes in pencil. Use the editing symbols in Chapter 2 or make up your own method.

5. Read as slowly as you can. Look at each word individually. If you are unsure whether a word is spelled correctly, check the dictionary.

6. Focus on catching mechanical errors, such as spelling or punctuation, but don't ignore larger changes that you think are necessary.

7. Make sure the first word in every sentence is capitalized and look especially closely at lists, quotations, and headings to make sure they follow the correct rules and are consistent in style.

8. You may want to use a computer spell checker before you print out a hard copy to work on yourself. However, be aware that most spell checkers are programmed for American spelling, which is slightly different from Canadian spelling.

CHECKLIST FOR PROOFREADING

Have I:	Help!
☑ Proofread for spelling errors, and checked my work against a list of common spelling mistakes?	
☑ Checked my work against a list of commonly confused words?	Commonly Confused Words, page 51
☑ Divided words at line endings only when necessary and in an appropriate place?	Word Division, page 67
☑ Used abbreviations that are appropriate to the type of writing I am doing?	Abbreviations, page 68
☑ Used a consistent style of numbering?	Numbers and Metric Units, page 69
☑ Used capital letters in appropriate places?	Capital Letters, page 71
☑ Indented every new paragraph?	
☑ Used correct punctuation?	Punctuation, page 73
☑ Used quotation marks around shorter quotations and indented quotations of longer than four lines?	Quotation Marks, page 78
☑ Acknowledged all outside sources properly?	Acknowledging Your Sources, page 125
☑ Identified titles of works using underlining, italics, or quotation marks, as necessary?	Quotation Marks, page 78 Italics and Underlining, page 82

Spelling:
Six Common Spelling
Questions Answered

Most "rules" in spelling have exceptions. The following guidelines can be useful, but when in doubt, always refer to a dictionary.

1. How do I know if a word is spelled *ie* or *ei*?
Learn this saying:

	Examples:
I before E	field, thief, believe, chief, friend
Except after C,	receive, ceiling, receipt, deceive
Or when sounded like A,	neighbour, freight, eight, sleigh
As in neighbour or weigh.	
Except seize and seizure,	
And also leisure,	
Weird, height, and either,	
Forfeit and neither.	

Be careful, as there are other exceptions (like *science* and *protein*)! The above rhyme can help you to remember the basic rule and some of the major exceptions.

2. How do I know when to drop the final -e if I am adding a suffix?
   a) Drop the final -e when the suffix to be added begins with a vowel.

   race + -ing   = racing
   love + -able   = lovable

   Except: Some words ending in -ce or -ge.

   province + -al   = provincial
   courage + -ous   = courageous

   b) Keep the final -e when the suffix to be added begins with a consonant.

   sincere + -ly   = sincerely
   arrange + -ment   = arrangement

   Except: argument, duly, ninth, truly

3. When do I double the final consonant if I am adding a suffix?
   a) Never double the final consonant when the suffix to be added begins with a consonant.

   commit + -ment   = commitment
   wet + -ness   = wetness

   b) Usually double the final consonant when the suffix to be added begins with a vowel.

   commit + -ing   = committing
   prefer + -ed   = preferred

   Except: If the accent is *not* on the last syllable, don't double the final consonant.

   benefit + -ed   = benefited
   profit + -ing   = profiting
   open + -ing   = opening

   Words ending in a single vowel and -l double the -l before a suffix that begins with a vowel.

   level + -ing   = levelling
   travel + -er   = traveller

4. When do I change the final -y to -i if I am adding a suffix?
   a) If the final -y follows a consonant, change the -y to -i.

   melody + -ous   = melodious
   baby + -s   = babies

   Except:

   pity + -ous   = piteous
   plenty + -ous   = plenteous

   b) If the final -y follows a vowel, keep the -y.

   play + -ed   = played
   donkey + -s   = donkeys

Except: Always keep the *-y* when adding *-ing*.
pray + -ing   = praying

5. What do I do when I add the suffix *-ly* to a word ending in *-l* already?

    Make no change. Just add *-ly*.
    wonderful + -ly   = wonderfully
    casual + -ly   = casually

6. When do I double the *-s* when adding *dis-* or *mis-* at the beginning of a word?

    Make no changes. Just add *dis-* or *mis-*.
    dis- + appear   = disappear
    mis- + spell   = misspell

    There are no exceptions!

Hyphenated Words   Here is a chart of the most common types of hyphenated words.

CATEGORY	KEY WORDS	EXAMPLES	RULE
Numbers	twenty-one	ninety-nine	Hyphenate compound numbers between twenty-one and ninety-nine.
	one-half	three-fourths, two-fifths, seven-eighths	Spelled-out fractions require a hyphen between numerator and denominator.
	two-metre wall	1000-m race, five-litre can	When a number + a unit of measure precedes a noun, put a hyphen between the number and the unit.
	eight-year-old girl	seventy-year-old school, a two-year-old	When writing a number + *year* + *old*, put a hyphen after the number and after *year*.
	one-thirty	five-fifteen, eight-twenty	When spelling out time, put a hyphen between the hour and the minutes.
	twelve-odd occasions	150-odd books, thirty-odd participants	When writing a number + *odd*, separate the two with a hyphen.
Commonly Hyphenated Prefixes	pro-American	pre-Christian, all-Canadian	When placing a prefix before a proper name, separate the two with a hyphen.

CATEGORY	KEY WORDS	EXAMPLES	RULE
	self-centred	self-control, self-confident	When combining *self* with another word, put a hyphen after *self*.
	all-seeing	all-powerful, all-knowing, *but* all right, almost	When combining *all* + another word, put a hyphen after *all*.
	half-baked	half-life, half-mast, *but* halfway	When combining *half* + another word, put a hyphen after *half*.
Family Relationships	sister-in-law	brothers-in-law, mother-in-law	When writing *in-law*, put a hyphen after the relationship word and after *in*.
	great-grandmother	great-aunt, great-great-grandfather	When writing of *great* family relationships, put a hyphen after each *great*.
Compound Modifiers Preceding the Word They Modify	thirst-quenching drink	Canadian-made piano, smoke-filled room, time-saving device	Hyphenate a combination of word + participle when the compound precedes a noun.
	well-known region	best-dressed entrant, ill-conceived plan, little-understood principle	Compound adjectives preceding a noun are hyphenated.
Clarifying Hyphens	Re-cover the chair after you've recovered from the accident.	I re-created the garden for recreation.	Hyphenate prefixes when confusion with other words is possible.
Cases in which No Hyphen is Needed	quickly finished job	beautifully executed jump, terribly confused speech	Compound modifiers with adverbs ending in *-ly* are never hyphenated.
	prewar	pre-, post-, over-, under-, intra-, extra-, sub-, super-, pro-, anti-, co-, non-, un-, semi-, supra-	Don't use a hyphen for any of these prefixes *except* when they are joined to a proper name.

▶ *Rewrite the following paragraphs, inserting hyphens as necessary.*

The Treetops Hotel is a very well known tourist attraction in Kenya. This five metre high hotel is built in a mgumu tree, right beside an all important watering hole for animals. In the past, the well heeled patrons of the hotel have included the twenty six year old daughter of King George VI, Elizabeth, along with the King's son in law, Philip. Elizabeth received the news of her father's death and her own ascension to the throne while staying at Treetops.

Be sure not to miss the late afternoon check in time; afterward, the stairs to the hotel are raised and, as the sun goes down, you can watch animals come out to drink at the pond below. But be careful: leaving your window even halfway open could mean that badly behaved monkeys will sneak in and steal the shiny necklace you inherited from your great grandmother!

WORD DIVISION (SYLLABICATION)

The best rule for word division is to avoid it if you can. When you do need to divide a word at the end of a line, here are some guidelines to follow.

1. Divide between syllables.

   Always divide between syllables. Check a dictionary if you are not sure of the correct place.

> Many word processing programs have a "hyphenate" command, which will divide words and insert hyphens at the end of a line for you. Be sure to check the word breaks, though. If any of them look odd, consult a dictionary.

2. Put the hyphen at the end of the line.

   Always place the hyphen at the end of the first line. Never begin a line with a hyphen.

   Avoid: A St. Thomas, Ontario, jewe
      -ller invented a painless way to pierce ears.
   Acceptable: A St. Thomas, Ontario, jewel-
      ler invented a painless way to pierce ears.

3. Do not divide short words.
   Avoid: a-way
        heav-y
   Acceptable: scien-tific
        philo-sophical

4. Divide already-hyphenated words only at the hyphen.
absent-minded
good-natured

5. Avoid dividing proper nouns.
Avoid: Minis-try of Health
Pauline Rabin-ovich

Acceptable: Ministry
of Health

Pauline
Rabinovich

Abbreviations Abbreviations should rarely be used in formal written assignments, especially where there may be confusion over their meaning.

Here are some common abbreviations that you should avoid in formal writing:

Avoid	*Acceptable*
etc.	and so on/and so forth
e.g.	for example
i.e.	that is
Xmas	Christmas
Sept. 14/53	14 September 1953
Fri., Sat.	Friday, Saturday
Eng., Hist.	English, History

Here are the five kinds of abbreviations that you can usually use in written work:

1. Before Proper Names
Abbreviate titles *before* proper names. The most common abbreviations are

Mr., Mrs., Ms., Dr., Messrs., Mme., M.

2. After Proper Names
Abbreviate titles and professional degrees *after* proper names. Some of the most common abbreviations are

Jr., Sr., B.A., M.D., Ph.D., D.D.S.

Do not use more than one abbreviation to convey the same meaning.

Avoid: Dr. N. Osborne, M.D.
Acceptable: Dr. N. Osborne
Acceptable: N. Osborne, M.D.

3. Agencies and Organizations
   Abbreviate names of government agencies and organizations when the abbreviations are more commonly used than the spelled-out names. Some examples are:

   R.C.M.P. NATO
   S.P.C.A. UNICEF
   UN   UNESCO

   The trend is toward omitting the periods in such abbreviations, but consult the dictionary to be sure.

4. "Saint"
   Abbreviate the word *Saint* when it is part of a place name.

   St. John's, Newfoundland
   St. Thomas, Ontario
   but Saint John, New Brunswick

5. Miscellaneous
   In certain kinds of papers and assignments, abbreviations of sums of money, times of the day, and units of measurement are accepted. As a rule of thumb, if there are a lot of such references in the paper, use an abbreviation.

   Money $41.75
   Time 9:30 a.m., 11:15 p.m.
          0930, 2315 (twenty-four-hour clock)
   Measurement 16 km, 454 t, 6 mL

> Do not use periods after metric symbols, unless they come at the ends of sentences.

Numbers and Metric Units

NUMBERS

In formal writing, numbers are generally spelled out unless a great many numbers are used in a single paper, such as a science paper. Here are three general rules for numbers:

1. Numbers Below 101
   Numbers below 101 are usually spelled out.
   Compound numbers between twenty-one and ninety-nine are hyphenated.

   ninety-six kilometres
   sixteen players
   135 cars

Note: Round numbers over 101 are usually spelled out. For example, *two hundred* books, *a thousand* people.

2. Numerals

Numerals may be used for dates, street numbers, room numbers, sums of money, telephone numbers, temperature readings, page numbers, numbered sections and chapters in books, statistics, and with a.m. and p.m. to indicate time.

> 11 February 1940 *or* 11/02/40
> 6622 Elmwood Avenue
> 25°C (*not* 25 degrees Celsius)
> page 92, Chapter III

3. Beginning a Sentence

When a number begins a sentence, it should be spelled out.

> *Two hundred and ninety-five* women and men sit in the House of Commons in Ottawa.

METRIC UNITS

The following chart outlines the metric units in everyday use.

QUANTITY	UNIT	SYMBOL
mass (weight)	gram (one-thousandth of a kilogram) kilogram tonne (one thousand kilograms)	g kg t
volume and capacity	cubic centimetre cubic metre millilitre (one-thousandth of a litre) centilitre (one-hundredth of a litre) litre	cm^3 m^3 mL cL L
length	millimetre (one-thousandth of a metre) centimetre (one-hundredth of a metre) metre kilometre (one thousand metres)	mm cm m km
area	hectare square centimetre square metre	ha cm^2 m^2
speed	metres per second kilometres per hour	m/s km/h
time	second minute hour	s min h
temperature	degree(s) Celsius	°C
pressure	pascal kilopascal (one thousand pascals)	Pa kPa

Keep the following points in mind when you use metric measurement:

1. Avoid mixing numerals and the full names of metric symbols.

    Avoid: I bought *3 kilograms* of meat.
    Acceptable: I bought *3 kg* of meat.
    Acceptable: I bought *three kilograms* of meat.

2. Avoid using a period after a metric symbol (unless the symbol is at the end of a sentence).

    Avoid: There are over *11 000 ha.* of wheat in Canada.
    Acceptable: There are over *11 000 ha* of wheat in Canada.

3. Use a hyphen between the numeral and the symbol when they are used as a modifier.

    Avoid: My car has a 300 cm^3 engine.
    Acceptable: My car has a 300-cm^3 engine.

4. Use decimals rather than fractions in metric units.

    Avoid: Joanne's height is 1 2/3 m.
    Acceptable: Joanne's height is 1.66 m.

Capital Letters

1. In General
    Capitalize the first word of a sentence, the pronoun *I*, and proper nouns.

EXAMPLE	CATEGORY
My father says I ought to improve my penmanship.	first word in sentence and pronoun *I*
Alice Munro, Fidel Castro, Bullwinkle	names of people and animals
Vancouver, Hudson Bay	geographical locations
Tuesday, June, New Year's Day	days, months, and holidays
Introduction to Basket Weaving 101	specific school courses
Canada Packers, Inc., Red Cross	names of companies and organizations
Irish, Caucasian, Yiddish	nationalities, races, and languages
Buddhism, Christianity	religions
CN Tower	buildings
10532 Hillside Avenue	parts of addresses

2. Direct Quotation
   Capitalize the first word in a direct quotation.

   > "Tomorrow morning," announced Ms. Williams, "we'll have a short test on long division."

   Note: The word *we'll* is not capitalized because it does not begin a sentence.

3. Historical
   Capitalize the names of historical events and documents.

   > Second World War, Charter of Rights and Freedoms

4. Titles
   Capitalize the first word and all important words in the titles of books, movies, plays, songs, articles, poems, and short stories.

   > *Paddle to the Amazon*, "An Ounce of Cure," *Attack of the Killer Tomatoes*

5. Letters
   Capitalize the first word in the salutation and closing of a letter.

   > Dear Abby, Dear Ms. Takahara, Yours truly, Sincerely

6. Titles Before Names
   Capitalize titles before the names of individuals.

   > Rabbi Morris, Ambassador Rodriguez, Ms. Geertz
   > Give the prescription to Doctor Piltz.

   Note: Titles that are used alone are not capitalized.

   > The doctor gave me a prescription.

7. Other
   Capitalize words like *father, mother,* and *aunt* and *uncle* when they are part of a person's name or when they are used in place of a person's name.

   > Tell me, Doctor, how long will my hand be in a cast?
   > My brother went looking for Uncle Mario.

Do not capitalize *north, south, west, east,* or any combination of these unless they are part of a proper name, such as *North York* or *South Dakota*. Do not capitalize the seasons: *spring, summer, fall, autumn, winter.*

▶ *Rewrite the following sentences, adding capitalization as necessary.*

"The canadian," wrote j.b. priestley in his introduction to *the bodley head leacock*, "is often a baffled man because he feels different from his british kindred and his american neighbours, sharply refuses to be lumped together with either of them, yet cannot make plain the difference." My mother is a muslim, born in pakistan; dad is a jewish rabbi, born in israel; i was born in normal, ohio; and we are all proud to call ourselves canadian. I have noticed that canadian patriotism is not usually expressed as allegiance to a flag, or to the constitution, as it is by americans. But every winter, we remember what draws us together, from north to south and east to west: the cold!

Punctuation

CROSS-REFERENCE

▶ For more information on abbreviations, see page 68.

PERIOD

The primary use of the period is to end statements or commands.

> "Googol" is the mathematical term for the number one followed by one hundred zeros.

> Memorize the symbols on the periodic table of the elements.

Periods are also frequently used in abbreviations.

> Do not use periods after metric symbols (for example, 10 mL, 31 m, 25 L). If a metric symbol is at the end of a sentence, there will be a period to close the sentence.
>
> > He ran 1500 m.

COMMA

Whenever you are unsure about comma usage, first check the rules in this section; however, "When in doubt, leave it out."

1. Lists
    Use a comma to separate the items in a series or list.

    > The Six Nations Confederacy includes the Cayuga, Mohawk, Oneida, Onondaga, Seneca, and Tuscarora.

    > The salami rolled out of the yard, between two parked cars, and onto the road.

> The comma before the conjunction, as in "... Seneca, and Tuscarora" is optional. But whichever method you choose, be consistent.

2. Introductory Words or Groups of Words
   a) Use a comma after introductory words such as "No,"
   "Well," "However," and so on.

   Well, did you feed my fish?
   Yes, I fed the fish to the cat.

   b) A phrase at the beginning of a sentence should be followed
   by a comma if it is long or if its meaning may be misunder-
   stood.

   Without waking from his sleep, José got in the car
   and drove across town.

   Hanging up, the coat looked limp and shapeless.

3. Words of Address
   Words of address should be set off by commas.

   Dino, did you understand that part about multiplying
   exponents?

   I didn't understand it at all, Mr. Laroche.

   Dear Santa,

4. Additional Information
   A comma should be used to mark off additional, but not
   essential, information about a noun that comes before the
   information.

   The vampire, who was new to the neighbourhood, held
   a get-acquainted barbecue.

5. Interruption of Thought
   Use a comma to mark the interruption of a thought by a par-
   enthetical expression that adds supplementary information or
   comments by the writer. In this case, the commas act in the
   same way as parentheses or brackets.

   A python, I am sure you will agree, makes an ideal pet
   for young children.

6. Conjunctions
   Use a comma before a conjunction (examples: *and, but, or*)
   that joins two parts of a long compound sentence.

   I threw a party last night, and this morning there were
   three strangers asleep in my bathtub.

QUESTION MARK

The question mark is used to end sentences that ask a question.

Where can I get a watermelon popsicle?

What is the meaning of life?

EXCLAMATION MARK

The exclamation mark is used after sentences to show surprise or strong feeling. Use this punctuation sparingly or it will lose its meaning.

Take off!

I can't believe you fed my fish to the cat!

COLON

The colon is not needed very often. Chiefly, it is used to introduce items or ideas.

1. Lists
   Use a colon to begin a list of items.

   Bring these items: a pen, a dead fish, a length of rope.

2. Quotations
   Use a colon to separate introductory words from a formal quotation that is a complete sentence.

   Stephen Leacock's most famous line is often quoted: "Lord Ronald said nothing; he flung himself from the room, flung himself upon his horse and rode madly off in all directions."

> The colon must follow an independent clause when it is used to begin a list or introduce a quotation.

---

3. Business Letters
   Use a colon after the greeting of a business letter.

   Dear Mrs. McDonnell:

   Dear Messrs. Adamson and Ohira:

4. Time
   When numerals are used to express time, use a colon to separate the hours and minutes.

   The bus leaves at 3:10 p.m.

5. Plays
   Use a colon between act and scene numbers of a play.

   Shakespeare's *Hamlet*, III:ii

6. The Bible
   Use a colon between chapter and verse number of the Bible.

   Genesis 2:17

7. References
   Use a colon between the volume and page numbers of a cited reference.

   Literary History of Canada, II:179

8. Subtitles
   Use a colon to introduce a subtitle of a book or article or to introduce a section in one of these.

   "New Zoos: Taking Down the Bars" (article)

SEMICOLON

A semicolon is a tricky piece of punctuation. It is often described as both a strong comma and a weak period because it is used to join and separate parts of a sentence. Since the usage of the semicolon cannot be clearly defined, it is used sparingly and usually only in formal writing.

1. A semicolon is used to connect two complete thoughts if no joining word (such as *and* or *but*) is used. The two thoughts should be closely related to each other. The second thought does not begin with a capital letter.

   The results of the experiment were disappointing; our attempt to turn ginger ale into oil had failed completely.

2. A semicolon can be used before joining words such as *however*, *consequently*, *therefore*, and *nevertheless*.

   When we got to the party, the door of the limousine wouldn't open; therefore, we all had to climb out of the window in our tuxedoes and evening dresses.

DASH

Use dashes sometimes in informal writing and in dialogue but rarely in formal writing. They should always be used sparingly. Use a dash *only* to mark a sudden change in sentence structure or a break in thought.

The NHL uses about 15 000 pucks a year—enough to form a stack 440 m high.

If your software does not allow you to type a dash, use two hyphens side by side.

CROSS-REFERENCE

▶ See *Hyphenated Words*, page 65 and *Word Division*, page 67.

HYPHEN

Use hyphens to divide a word at the end of a line and to spell certain words correctly.

APOSTROPHE

The apostrophe shows possession and replaces missing letters in contractions.

1. Possession
   a) To show possession of singular nouns, add -'s.

      the school's book
      Marco's speech

   b) To show possession of plural nouns *not* ending in -s, add -'s.

      the men's department
      the mice's tails

   c) To show possession of plural nouns ending in -s, add only an apostrophe.

      the boys' books (more than one book, belonging to more than one boy)

      the teachers' lounge (one lounge belonging to more than one teacher)

   d) *Do not* use an apostrophe or an -'s to show possession for the pronoun *who* or for personal pronouns. Here is a list of these pronouns with their correct possessive forms:

Pronouns	*Possessive*
I	mine
you	yours
he, she, it	his, hers, its
we	ours
you	yours
they	theirs
who	whose
but	
one	one's
everybody	everybody's

2. Contractions
   An apostrophe used in a contraction marks where one or more letters have been removed. Avoid contractions in formal

writing, but feel free to use them in informal writing and in dialogue.

Here are some common contractions. The apostrophe replaces the underlined letter.

do n<u>o</u>t	don't
can<u>not</u>	can't
should <u>have</u>	should've
it <u>is</u>	it's
who <u>is</u>	who's

TRY IT!

▶ *Rewrite the following paragraphs, inserting apostrophes as necessary.*

Have you ever had the urge to cut your hair after breaking up with someone or before turning over a new leaf? Its a common way to express either a new beginning or a renunciation of something. In fact, in most cultures, hair is a symbol of power, intellect, and the life force.

Think about it: why is a soldiers hair cut so short when he enlists? What do monks tonsures signify? Why was the sixties style of long hair considered so rebellious? What does a skinheads baldness symbolize?

In the Old Testament story of Samson and Delilah, Samsons hair gives him superhuman strength—until Delilah cuts it off. In Greek mythology, Medusas hair is made of snakes. One look at her and you turned to stone; thats what you call a bad hair day.

QUOTATION MARKS

Quotation marks separate someone's exact words from the body of the work. Here are some of their more common uses:

1. Direct Speech
    Quotation marks are used to mark off a speaker's exact words. Use them only for direct speech, not indirect reports of what someone said.

    Direct Speech: Mulder said, "My sister was abducted by aliens!"

    Indirect Speech: Mulder said that his sister was abducted by aliens.

    If the direct speech asks a question, put the question mark inside the quotation marks.

    Mulder said, "Do you think my sister was abducted by aliens?"

If the entire sentence asks a question, put the question mark outside the quotation marks. (You don't need a period inside the quotation.)

Did Mulder say, "My sister was abducted by aliens"?

2.   Dialogue
You can also use quotation marks to distinguish the exact words of different speakers in a conversation. The following passage illustrates most of the rules for punctuating dialogue.

New sentence follows. Use a period.

"There's no one home," she said when she saw his intentions. "They weren't expecting me this time, and presumably, they weren't expecting you either."

Whole sentence is a question. Question mark goes inside quotation mark.

"Then it is the right house?" Desmond said. Stupidly, he thought. Right house for what?

New paragraph for each new speaker.

Part of the same sentence— use a comma.

But she seemed to understand. "Oh, yes. It's the right house. Some day the city will get around to putting a plaque on the wall but for the time being I prefer it the way it is. My name, by the way," she added, "is Mary Brennan. I don't live here but I stop by often enough. The old man, you see, was one of my teachers years ago."

Each speech must begin and end with quotation marks.

From "The Leper's Squint" in *The Barclay Family Theatre* by Jack Hodgins. © 1981. Reprinted by permission of Macmillan Canada.

If a speaker's words go on for more than one paragraph, begin each new paragraph with a quotation mark, but put a closing quotation mark only at the end of the last paragraph of the whole quotation.

"It was not much of a dog," he explained, sitting up. "It was only a little one, half—no, almost wholly—starved. But its manners were good. At one time it had been, I am sure, someone's pet, sleek, fat, probably impertinent. When I saw it, its coat was ragged and its ears were torn and its ribs were there to count.

"It was on the first morning that it found me. I was, you must understand, carrying a message for the Underground, and it was imperative that that message reach one man, the right man."

From "The Czech Dog," by W. G. Hardy. © 1945 by W. G. Hardy.

3.   Quotations in an Essay
Use quotation marks in your essays to enclose words that come directly from another writer or speaker. You will probably use them in research papers or if you quote authors in an English essay. Try to work shorter quotations into the body of the paper. Here are some examples of how to do that:

Why have the blues become so popular in the latter half of the twentieth century? Perhaps because, with the amount of alienation and rootlessness in modern society, "all of us are beginning to experience the melancholic dissatisfaction that weighed upon the hearts of the black people of the Mississippi Delta, the land where the blues began" (Lomax ix).

Why have the blues become so popular in the latter half of the twentieth century? According to Alan Lomax, it is because the alienation and rootlessness in modern society is similar to "the melancholic dissatisfaction that weighed upon the hearts of the black people of the Mississippi Delta, the land where the blues began" (ix).

Why have the blues become so popular in the latter half of the twentieth century? One commentator (Lomax ix) suggests that modern experience of alienation and rootlessness makes it easier for us to understand "the melancholic dissatisfaction" that characterized the lives of poor southern blacks in "the land where the blues began."

4. Long Quotations
"Long" means more than four lines. Instead of using quotation marks, indent a longer quotation five spaces from the left-hand margin, and single space it.

In *The Land Where the Blues Began*, musicologist Alan Lomax describes the growing popularity of the music known as the blues over the course of the twentieth century:

In order to hear the blues, when I was very young, my girlfriend and I slipped into the black ghetto of my Southern hometown under the cover of darkness. If we'd been caught there, we would probably have been expelled from the university. Nowadays everyone sings and dances to bluesy music, and the mighty river of the blues uncoils in the ear of the planet. Indeed, the blues may have become the best-known tune humans have ever sung. (1)

5. Quotation Within a Quotation
If the original writer whom you are quoting has already included quoted material in a sentence, change the original quotation marks to single quotation marks and use regular quotation marks to enclose the passage as a whole.

Lomax's book contains innumerable comments and anecdotes from great bluesmen, which add colour to his treatment of the subject: "Leadbelly once told me, 'When you lie down at night, turning from side to side, and you can't be satisfied no way you do, Old Man Blues got you.'"

6. Titles
Quotation marks are used to enclose the titles of magazine and newspaper articles, book chapters, poems, songs, short stories, and essays.

"The Reincarnation of Ling"	(magazine article)
Chapter 3, "How to be a Rocket Scientist"	(book chapter)
"Thirty Below"	(poem title)
"O Canada"	(song title)

Note: titles of plays, books, films, TV series, magazines, newspapers, and works of art are set in italics or underlined.

7. Words as Words
Use quotation marks to draw attention to specific words.

> Some Canadians have a tendency to end every sentence with "eh."

> You can use underlining or italics in place of quotation marks to draw attention to a specific word. Be consistent. Choose one method and stick to it.

PARENTHESES

Parentheses are used to enclose supplementary explanations and comments so that they don't get confused with the overall flow of thought. Use parentheses as little as possible in school assignments.

1. Within a Sentence
If the parentheses appear within a sentence, don't begin the material inside the parentheses with a capital letter. Put the period outside the last parenthesis, since it ends the whole sentence, not just the material inside.

> He handed me a bowl full of a grey, gelatinous mass (actually, oatmeal) that looked like jellied dishwater.

> The scream carried down the length of the alley and reverberated against the metal sides of the overflowing garbage bins (the garbage strike had been dragging on for weeks).

2. Between Sentences
If the parentheses contain an entire sentence between two other sentences, put the period *inside* the final parenthesis, and start the sentence with a capital letter.

> I have a picture of you beside my desk. (It's the one of you wearing your fuzzy rabbit slippers, with a lampshade on your head.) Whenever I look at it, it reminds me of all the good times we had last summer.

SQUARE BRACKETS

Use square brackets to add editorial comments to quotations, such as changing a word or two in the quotation so that it reads properly or adding information such as names and dates.

> Children [in Japan] are put under incredible pressure to perform, beginning in kindergarten and continuing right through high school. That's because their future opportunities depend so much on which university accepts them. [Japanese teacher Toshiko] Toriyama told me the system is so rigid that by the third week in grade 1 a child must have reached a specified page in a textbook.
>
> From "A Gifted Teacher in Japan," in *Inventing the Future*, by David Suzuki. Reprinted with permission of Stoddart Publishing Co. Limited.

ELLIPSIS MARKS

Ellipsis marks are three spaced periods that show that something has been left out of a quotation. The omitted part may be as short as a single word or as long as several sentences. Be careful not to use ellipsis marks to alter the original meaning of a quotation.

Full Quotation: "The once-plentiful bull trout, so-called because of the shape of its head, is beginning to make a comeback in the rivers of Alberta."

Shortened Version Using Ellipsis Marks: "The once-plentiful bull trout . . . is beginning to make a comeback in the rivers of Alberta."

If you add ellipsis marks at the end of a sentence, include an extra period. That is, instead of three ellipsis marks, use four.

Italics and Underlining

Use italic type on a computer wherever you would use underlining in a longhand or typewritten document.

1. Titles
   Underline the titles of books, magazines, newspapers, plays, TV series, and movies, as well as the names of specific ships or planes.

Colombo's Concise Canadian Quotations	(book)
Harrowsmith	(magazine)
The Calgary Herald	(newspaper)
Napoleon	(play)
The Nature of Things	(TV series)
Breakfast at Tiffany's	(movie)
H.M.S. Queen Elizabeth II	(ship)

2. Emphasis
   Use italics (or underlining) instead of an exclamation mark to emphasize a specific word in a sentence.

   I most certainly do *not* want a surprise party on my birthday (which is on Friday), even though I will be out until 8:00 p.m. that night, and will be leaving my key under the mat.

3. Foreign Words
   Underline or italicize foreign words and phrases. If you are not sure whether a word is considered foreign, check a dictionary.

   There is nothing wrong with guns *per se*; it is what comes out of them that worries me.

FORMATTING
FORMAT YOUR FINAL DRAFT

CROSS-REFERENCE

▶ Refer to the overview of the writing process on page 11.

GOAL: *To finalize the layout and add front and back matter to your work.* Whether you are writing your essay on a computer, on a typewriter, or by hand, follow these rules.

- Use standard-sized white paper: blank for typed or printed work and lined if you are writing by hand.

- Leave a 3-cm margin all round. (If you are working on computer, leave the margins at the default setting.)

- Leave one line space between each line of writing.

- Indent each paragraph.

- Use one side of the paper only.

- Put a heading in the top right-hand corner of each page except the first, indicating your name, the teacher's name, the title of the work, and the date.

> If you are using a computer, you can put the title, date, your name, and your teacher's name in a "header." The computer will then add that information to the top of every page of your file.

Formatting on the Computer

A computer can help you create a very polished presentation. Most word processing programs allow you to use different styles and sizes of fonts, or typefaces, as well as boldface, italics, and boxes to add a professional look to your writing. It is easy to get carried away by the possibilities. Go ahead and experiment, but take note of the following guidelines.

Fonts Fonts are typefaces. You can vary the style and the size of your fonts in most word processing programs.

- Choose a font that is easy to read for the body of the text. Times, Helvetica, or Palatino are good choices.

- You can use a different font for headings (if your writing has any), but don't use a separate font for every level of subhead. Stick to one that you like, and vary the size of the type (or use italics) to indicate the different subheads.

- Font sizes are measured in points. Use 12-point type for the body of the text (or 10-point, if you are really pressed for space). Set the title in larger type, but don't go any higher than 24 points. For headings and subheads, try 14 points and 12 points.

SOME TYPICAL FONTS

Courier
Helvetica
Palatino
Times

Font Sizes

10 point 12 point 14 point 18 point 24 point

Headings and Titles Here are some tips for making headings and titles easy to spot.

1. If the title is on a separate title page, centre it horizontally, and use a larger type size—perhaps 14 or 18 points.

2. Distinguish between levels of heads and subheads as well. You can do this in several ways.

   - By altering the space between the heading and the text that follows (the more space you leave, the more important the heading appears).

   - By altering the font size (the larger the font size, the more important the heading).

   - By capitalizing all the letters in important headings and only the first letter of each word in subheads.

   - By using boldface, italics, and underlining appropriately. A bold heading will usually look more important than one that is not bold, and an underlined heading is usually more important than one that is not underlined.

3. As far as possible, use parallel construction in your headings. For example, if one of your headings is "Preparing the Canvas," don't make the next one "Begin to Paint." Instead, it should read "Beginning to Paint."

Boxes Putting an outline around a group of words is a good way to draw attention to them. However, don't use boxes or outlines when you are writing essays. The important points should emerge clearly from the way you write and structure your argument, rather than from the page layout.

Lists Try to be as consistent as possible in the way you present your lists. Here are some points to watch for:

1. Use a colon or a period in the sentence before the list, but try to use the same punctuation each time.

2. If each item in the list is a sentence fragment or a single word, you may begin each item with a lower case letter. For complete sentences, begin with a capital.

3. Be consistent in your end punctuation as well. Some options include the following:

   • End each item with a period (especially if each is a full sentence).

   • Put no punctuation at the end of the sentence.

   • Use semicolons or commas at the end of all items, followed by the word *and* at the end of the second-to-last item, and a period at the end of the last item.

     Three of the most popular fitness activities are
     - walking,
     - running, and
     - swimming.

4. Use numbers for sequential items (for example, a set of instructions). For other types of lists, you can use numbers, bullets (•), letters, or some other appropriate marker.

VISUAL AIDS

Illustrations, figures, and tables can be a big help in clarifying written information. Here are some tips on how to incorporate visual aids into your work.

Figures

Figures are maps, graphs, illustrations, tables, and diagrams that are used to convey information. Refer to each figure at an appropriate place in your paper, and then insert the figure into the text, as close as possible to the text reference (but not before it).

Whenever possible, place visual aids at the top or bottom of a page. It is much easier to estimate how much space to leave when you do not have text above and below. Besides, this layout usually looks better.

If you want to include figures in your paper, here is how it's done:

1. Give each figure a title and a number. Capitalize the first letter of all the important words. If you are writing on computer, put the figure number and title in boldface or italics.

   Figure 1: Projected Annual Availability of Water Per Person in 2000

2. Place the figure at the top or bottom of a page, as close as possible to the first text reference to it (but never before this first reference). If you are writing on computer, but your figure drawing is not on disk, be sure to leave enough space to paste the artwork in, leaving at least an inch of space above and below the figure.

3. If you copied the figure, or got the idea for it from somewhere outside your own head, you need to acknowledge your source. Place the complete source at the bottom of the figure:

   Source: World Health Organization (WHO), *Evaluation of the Strategy for Health for All by the Year 2000* (Geneva, Switzerland: WHO, 1987), Table 19, p. 72.

4. If your teacher requires that you include a table of figures, write out the number, title, and page number of each figure, and insert it on the page following the table of contents.

   Here is a figure presented within the body of a paper:

Figure 1 shows that although 70 percent of the earth's surface is covered by water, only a small percentage of that amount is fresh water. Most of that is frozen in glaciers, making it inaccessible. In fact, only about one percent of the world's fresh water supplies are readily accessible.

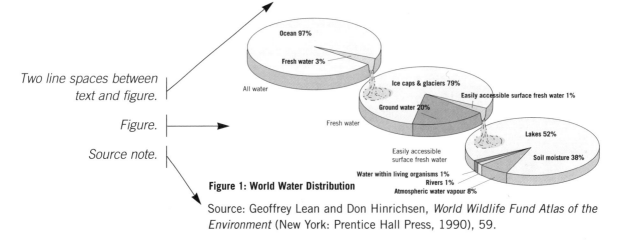

Two line spaces between text and figure.

Figure.

Source note.

Figure 1: World Water Distribution

Source: Geoffrey Lean and Don Hinrichsen, *World Wildlife Fund Atlas of the Environment* (New York: Prentice Hall Press, 1990), 59.

Graphs   A graph is a type of figure. Graphs are very useful when you need to present statistical data in a way that makes them easy to understand. Follow the format for figures explained in the previous section.

Here are three common types of graphs and when to use them.

1. Circle or Pie Graph
    Use pie graphs to illustrate percentages. You need to have percentages that add up to 100 to make this type of graph. If you don't know all the percentages, or if only one portion is relevant, you can designate the remaining portion of the pie as "Other."

    To create wedges of the right size, multiply the percentage you want to illustrate by 360°. This gives you the number of degrees for the wedge. Use a protractor to measure out the right angle.

How Often Do Canadians Buy Lottery Tickets?

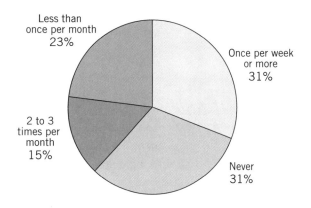

2. Line Graph
    Use line graphs like the one below to show trends.

Concentration of Airborne Lead, 1972 to 1982

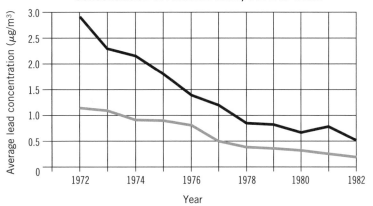

3. Bar Graph
Bar graphs are useful when you want to compare. You can also use them to show trends.

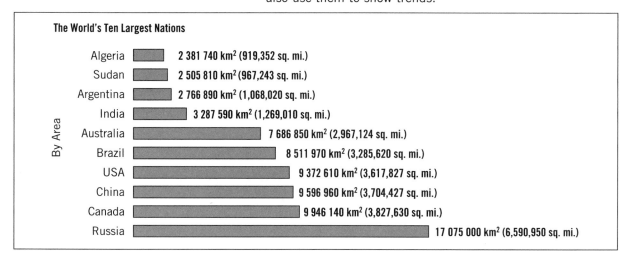

The World's Ten Largest Nations

By Area		
Algeria		2 381 740 km² (919,352 sq. mi.)
Sudan		2 505 810 km² (967,243 sq. mi.)
Argentina		2 766 890 km² (1,068,020 sq. mi.)
India		3 287 590 km² (1,269,010 sq. mi.)
Australia		7 686 850 km² (2,967,124 sq. mi.)
Brazil		8 511 970 km² (3,285,620 sq. mi.)
USA		9 372 610 km² (3,617,827 sq. mi.)
China		9 596 960 km² (3,704,427 sq. mi.)
Canada		9 946 140 km² (3,827,630 sq. mi.)
Russia		17 075 000 km² (6,590,950 sq. mi.)

> Use a computer drawing program to create figures of all kinds. Some software allows you to translate data into pie graphs, line graphs, or bar graphs with the click of a button.

ADDING FRONT AND BACK MATTER

Now it is time to prepare the front and back matter for your finished work. You will not always need to include all of these elements. The best way to decide which are needed is to ask. For a school assignment, check with your teacher; for business reports, ask to see a copy of a previous report.

Title Page

In most cases, your writing will need some kind of title. For a short piece, you can put the title at the top of the page. For most longer pieces, you will need to add a separate title page. If you are writing an assignment, check with your teacher to see if she or he has a preference.

• Capitalize all the important words in a title. Usually, you don't have to capitalize smaller words such as *a*, *the*, *to*, *for*, *in*, etc. unless they are the first word in the title.

• Don't put a period at the end of the title.

• Don't underline the title. However, you may want to use boldface type in a larger point size if you are writing on a computer.

CROSS-REFERENCE

▶ For information on how to present an essay, see page 99; for a research paper, see page 136; for a business report, see page 156.

> Although paragraphs are generally indented on the first line, you may choose not to indent the first paragraph of your work. For school assignments, ask your teacher if this format is acceptable.

Here are three examples of how to write a title. The first two are for essays; the third is for a business report.

Sample 1: Title for a short essay.

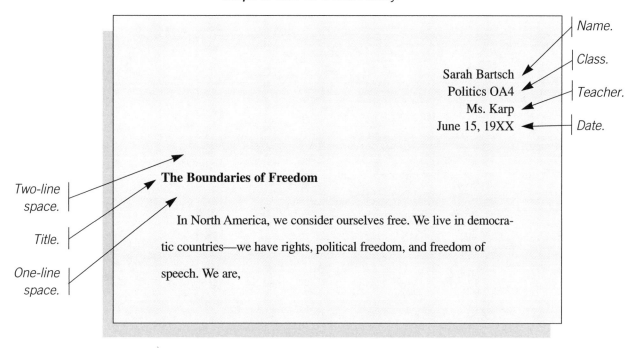

Name.

Class.

Teacher.

Date.

Sarah Bartsch
Politics OA4
Ms. Karp
June 15, 19XX

Two-line space.

Title.

One-line space.

The Boundaries of Freedom

In North America, we consider ourselves free. We live in democratic countries—we have rights, political freedom, and freedom of speech. We are,

Sample 2: Separate title page for a longer essay or research paper.

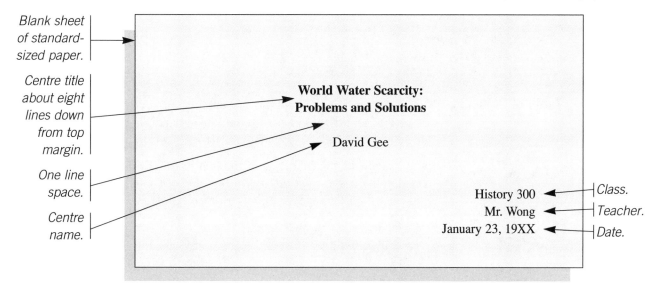

Blank sheet of standard-sized paper.

Centre title about eight lines down from top margin.

One line space.

Centre name.

World Water Scarcity: Problems and Solutions

David Gee

History 300
Mr. Wong
January 23, 19XX

Class.
Teacher.
Date.

Sample 3: Title page for a formal business report.

Office Safety Procedures ← Centre title about eight lines down from top margin.

← Blank sheet of standard-sized paper.

Prepared by

Abdul Kareem ← Two line spaces.

AK Office Inspection and Security ← Centre name of author.

← Four line spaces.

Prepared for

Harold Balkis, Manager ← Centre name of company and/or individual report is addressed to.

PCL Chemical Co. Ltd.

December 12, 19XX ← Date.

Table of Contents You only need to include a table of contents if the piece of writing has several sections and each section has a head. If you do include a table of contents, place it immediately after the title page.

Page 1 is always the first page of the text itself. If you need to refer to something in the front matter in the table of contents, count forward from the title page, and use a Roman numeral.

> Never put a number on the title page, and only put numbers on front matter that is referred to in the table of contents.

Here is how a table of contents should look:

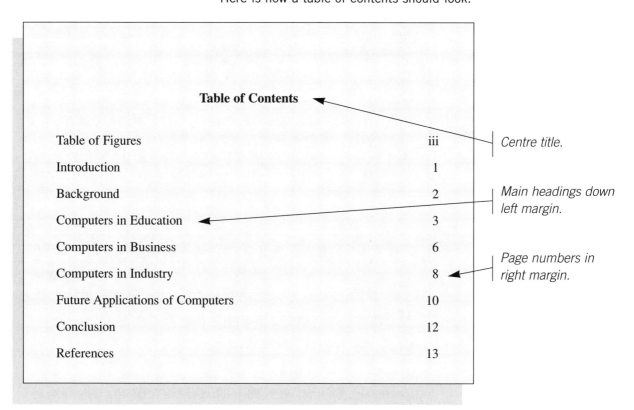

Table of Contents

Centre title.

Main headings down left margin.

Page numbers in right margin.

Table of Figures   If your paper includes a lot of figures or graphs, include a separate table listing them. Put it on a separate sheet, on the page following the table of contents. Follow exactly the same format as for the table of contents, listing each figure by name in order of appearance, and including a page number at the right-hand margin for each entry.

> Prepare the table of contents and table of figures after you have recopied or printed out the final version of your paper. That way, you can be sure the page numbers will not change.

Works Cited List and/or Bibliography

If you have used any outside sources in preparing your essay, you need to acknowledge them in the body of the text and in a list at the end of the paper. The proper format for works cited lists and bibliographies is covered in Chapter 5.

Appendices

Appendices contain information that is either too detailed or too long to include in the body of the paper. Supporting documents, long tables, and other background information can be placed at the back of the paper and labelled Appendix A, Appendix B, etc. Be sure you refer to each appendix at an appropriate point in the text, so your reader knows the information is available.

CROSS-REFERENCE

▶ See *Acknowledging Your Sources*, page 125.

FORMATTING CHECKLIST

Have I:

- ☑ Printed my work on clean white paper?
- ☑ Double spaced between each line?
- ☑ Left a 3-cm margin all round?
- ☑ Included a title, either at the top of the first page or on a separate title page?
- ☑ Included a header at the top of each page after the first?
- ☑ Numbered each page of text?
- ☑ Made sure that all the elements of the work are in place, including (if required) a table of contents, table of figures, list of references, and any appendices or intext figures and tables?
- ☑ Made sure I have complied with all the specific formatting requirements for this piece of writing?
- ☑ Used a consistent format for all lists and headings?

CHAPTER 4

WRITING ESSAYS

▶ **E**ssays allow you to express your point of view, your insights, or your opinion on a topic. Writing develops your writing skill and your ability to present your own ideas and arguments. This chapter includes several sample essays written by students and gives pointers on how to write them yourself.

CONTENTS

APPLYING THE WRITING PROCESS

ACTIVITY	TIPS AND TECHNIQUES	WHERE TO LOOK
Find and limit your topic	Even if you are using a topic suggested by your teacher, you may need to limit the topic in order to deal with it effectively in the allotted space.	Find and Limit Your Topic, page 11
Define your purpose and audience	Often the purpose of your essay is suggested by key words in the assignment. Use the list of key words in this chapter to help clarify exactly what you are being asked to do. For a school essay, your audience is usually your teacher.	Define Your Purpose and Audience, page 13 Key Words Used in Essay Topics, page 95
Gather your thoughts	Essays sometimes require a bit of research, but most of the ideas will be your own.	Gather Your Thoughts, page 13
Organize your ideas	For longer essays, an outline or tree diagram is usually a good idea.	Prepare an Outline or Tree Diagram, page 15
Write a draft	Your introduction should include a thesis statement. Each paragraph in the body of the essay relates back to the thesis statement.	The Parts of an Essay, page 95 Developing a Thesis Statement, page 96
Revise for organization, content, and focus		Revising, page 22
Edit paragraphs, sentences, and words		Editing, page 25
Proofread for spelling, punctuation, and grammar		Chapter 3
Format the final draft	Depending on the length and type of essay, as well as the standards expected by your audience (teacher), you may need to include elements such as a title page, table of contents, and list of figures.	Presenting an Essay, page 99

ESSAYS

An essay is a series of paragraphs that develops a topic and expresses the writer's viewpoint on that topic. No matter what kind of essay you are writing, the hard work will come in deciding what your point of view is and selecting information to back it up. Each paragraph has its own main idea, body, and conclusion, but at the same time, it is part of either the introduction, body, or conclusion of the essay. Whenever you introduce a new idea, you start a new paragraph.

Key Words Used in Essay Topics

Analyze Divide something into parts in order to understand the relationship both of the parts to each other and of the parts to the whole.

Argue Make a statement or express an opinion and support it with evidence or information.

Contrast Bring out the points of difference.

Compare Bring out the points of similarity and difference.

Criticize State your opinion of the correctness or merits of an item or issue. (May involve approval, disapproval, or both.)

Debate Consider, discuss, or argue the affirmative or negative sides of a proposition.

Define Give the meaning of a word or concept by placing it in the class to which it belongs and setting it off from other items in the same class.

Describe Give an account of; tell about; give a word picture of the topic.

Discuss Examine, analyze carefully, formulate a thesis, and give reasons pro and con.

Evaluate Give the good points and the bad; appraise; give an opinion regarding the value of; explore the advantages and disadvantages of the statement.

Explain Make clear; interpret; make plain; tell how to do something; tell the meaning of the topic.

Review An explanatory or critical account of a book, movie, etc.

THE PARTS OF AN ESSAY

Introduction

You will use your first paragraph (or sometimes the first two) to introduce the topic. A good introduction will tell readers what to expect in the body of the essay and make them want to read more. Your introduction should also describe your topic and point of view and anticipate the main points you will make in the body of your essay; it presents your thesis statement.

#1 - catch the reader
#2 - THESIS
#3 - Support thesis
#4 - △/ PROVE
#5 - △
#6 - Conclusion
(wrap up)

Creating Interest Try using one of the following approaches to liven up your introduction.

an anecdote

✓ a shocking statistic

✓ a question

a challenge

one person's experience

✓ a quotation

a joke

a description (of a place, situation, person, etc.)

Thesis Statement   A thesis statement describes your angle on the topic. Everything you write should relate back to your thesis sentence. For example, if your topic is "Cloning" you could use any of the following as your thesis sentence:

- Cloning opens up new frontiers in biotechnology never before reached by scientists. (The essay will attempt to persuade the reader that cloning is good.)

- This new cloning technology gives rise to three main ethical issues, which must be resolved before further progress is made. (The essay will set forth and describe the three issues.)

- Cloning of human embryos must be made illegal now, before the technology gets out of control. (The essay will encourage readers to act to stop human cloning.)

Here are some points to remember when you write a thesis statement:

- Don't use an obvious fact or statistic as your thesis sentence. Try to make a more general statement and use facts (if you want) to back it up. For example, the statement "Wayne Gretzky makes over $8 million a year" is not a good thesis statement because it is too specific. However, you could say "The salaries paid to sports figures are way too high." Even better, you could say "The salaries paid to top athletes are too high, and cannot be justified economically, socially, or morally." That way, your readers know that they can expect you to discuss each of these three aspects of the issue.

- Don't make broad generalizations unless you are prepared to back them up. Usually, the broader the statement, the harder it is to support it. If you say, "Cloning is wrong," you had better be sure your argument covers *all* cases where cloning might be practised, not just a few hand-picked scenarios.

• Keep your thesis statement handy. Write a sentence expressing your purpose, audience, and thesis. Keep this statement posted above your computer or by your desk so you can refer to it when you are writing.

T R Y I T !

▶ *Choose three of the following topics and write at least two different possible thesis sentences for each.*
1. boxing
2. capital punishment
3. affirmative action programs
4. the building of the Canadian National Railway
5. censorship
6. turnips
7. animal rights
8. advertising

> It is often easier to write your introduction last, after you know exactly what you have written.

In addition to presenting your thesis statement, you may use your introduction to summarize the main ideas you will be discussing. Here is a sample introduction for an essay on the Long March.

Thesis sentence.

Summary of three main themes in the essay.

The Long March remains one of the most integral factors in the survival and eventual victory of the Chinese Communist Party.① The discipline and hardship endured by approximately 100 000 Chinese communist men and women provided many of them later with the strength of mind and will to firmly redirect the course of Chinese history.② The experience of having overcome danger and death through critical decision making brought legitimacy and respect for future communist leaders who were veterans of the March.③ It also secured the supremacy of Mao Tse-Tung, the leader of the March.

The Body

Each paragraph in the body of your essay will relate back to your thesis, either directly or indirectly. Start a new paragraph for each main idea you use to support your thesis. Depending on the length of your essay, you may cover each main point in a single paragraph, or you might have to break it down, using separate paragraphs for each idea, example, anecdote, etc. that supports your main ideas.

The sample introduction above tells us that the essay will explain the importance of the Long March for the success of the Chinese

Communist Party. We can guess that it will probably contain a section on each of the following aspects:

1. how the March influenced the people who were on it to redirect the course of Chinese history;

2. how it made other people respect the communist leaders who had been on the March; and

3. how it secured the supremacy of Mao Tse-Tung.

We might also expect to find a bit of background on the March itself, depending on who the intended audience of the paper is.

The Conclusion   Your conclusion should restate what you have just told your readers and draw some conclusion from it. Usually, your conclusion will be one or two paragraphs at the end of the essay. Try to end on a positive note, and never introduce new facts, ideas, or arguments in the conclusion. Here are some ideas to help you end with a bang (you can also use any of the ideas suggested for livening up your introduction).

show how all your main ideas point to your thesis

harken back to a story or anecdote mentioned in the introduction

suggest a solution

look to the future

anticipate (and counter) any negative reactions to your ideas

call to action

> Avoid using the same wording in both your introduction and conclusion. Although they should say essentially the same thing, try to word your conclusion differently.

Now, here is the conclusion to the Long March essay.

There is no question that the Long March affected many aspects of Chinese society. It gave China a brilliant, perceptive leader, it unified the CCP and helped to assert China's independence. Although it is not the only reason for these changes, it was a very influential factor. So influential, in fact, that it would be safe to assume that China today would be a very different place were it not for the Long March of these men and women.

PRESENTING AN ESSAY

All essays need a title. If the essay is longer than two pages, make a separate title page, as shown in Chapter 3.

Make sure that you have acknowledged the sources of any quotations, diagrams, figures, statistics, and important ideas that are not your own.

SAMPLE ESSAYS

The three sample essays on the following pages differ according to each writer's purpose. If your essay topics are assigned by the teacher, look for any key words in the assignment. Then you can turn to the sample essay that is closest to the type you have to write, and use it as a model.

SAMPLE ESSAY #1

Are those who have the vote more free than those who have a job? Discuss the notion of freedom in Western society.

The key word in this topic is "discuss." When you are asked to *discuss* a topic, you are expected to examine it from various angles, present both sides of the issue, and come up with a conclusion based on the discussion.

The tone of the essay is serious, and it is written in a formal style.

Let's look at the sample essay paragraph by paragraph.

THE INTRODUCTION (first paragraph) introduces the topic by comparing North American freedom with Chinese freedom, suggesting that there is more than one way to define the concept. The thesis statement is "freedom is difficult to define, and ... our freedom can be limited in a variety of ways."

THE BODY (paragraphs 2 and 3) looks more closely at the costs and benefits of the Western emphasis on individual rights. The author has chosen to develop her thesis by comparing the pros and cons of freedom in North American and Chinese societies. She has arranged her ideas by order of importance (from most important to least important).

THE CONCLUSION (paragraphs 4 and 5) presents the opinion the writer has formed as a result of the discussion: The ideal for society is to find a healthy balance between rights and responsibilities.

Sarah Bartsch
Politics OA4
Ms. Karp
June 15, 19XX

The Boundaries of Freedom

In North America, we consider ourselves free. We live in democratic countries—we have rights, political freedom, and freedom of speech. We are, however, living in troubled economic times, and our foremost concern is survival. In China, the economy is flourishing and the unemployment rate is low. Chinese citizens, however, are not considered free by Western standards. Are those who have the vote more free than those who have a job? This is a difficult question that illustrates that freedom is difficult to define and that our freedom can be limited in a variety of ways.

In the West, we have freedom to pursue our own interests, and there is room for the creative and ambitious to thrive. The emphasis is on individualism, and individual rights are fiercely defended. This outlook, however, has led to fragmentation, for people do not realize the need to make sacrifices and to compromise for the benefit of the group. A classic example of this is the failure to devise a new Canadian Constitution. To achieve a greater degree of stability for our nations, democratic citizens must come to realize that sometimes we must put the welfare of the group ahead of what we consider to be our personal rights and freedoms.

Although we enjoy many rights and privileges, there are other ways in which our freedom is limited in North America. Our government is representative, not participatory, which limits the amount of input we have, weakening our sense of personal responsibility. Our vast media network influences the way we think and the values we hold from the day we are born. Stereotypes and narrow-mindedness prevent individuals from reaching their potential. Finally, in a capitalist society, an inevitable consequence is that a portion of the population will be kept in poverty—unemployed and unfulfilled.

While individualism forms the basis in western, democratic countries, it is a collective ideology that prevails in the Asia-Pacific nations. In these societies, individuals put their interest aside for their community, and the result is stability and order. Unfortunately, because of the social stigma attached to individuality, creativity and originality are stifled.

No matter into what circumstances we are born, it is our personal responsibility to follow a set of values, social norms, and laws. In doing so, we are in a sense losing some of our freedom, but it is necessary to follow these for they provide safety and security. Barriers of different degrees and forms exist in different cultures and societies, and no matter where we live, we can be sure that in one way or another, our freedom will be limited. "Man is born free, and everywhere is in chains" (Rousseau 3). The best we can do is to wisely use what freedom we have, to expand our freedom through education, and to strive for excellence. As a nation, we need to aim towards "a healthy fusion of the Western emphasis on individual rights, and the Asia-Pacific on collective responsibilities" (Dyer).

WORKS CITED

Dyer, Gwyn. "Asian nations have more to teach us than economics." *The Toronto Star*
  24 November 1993: A27.

Rousseau, Jean Jacques. *The Social Contract*. Ed. Lester G. Crocker. New York: Washington
  Square Press, 1967.

SAMPLE ESSAY #2

Compare the characters of Emma Bovary in Flaubert's *Madame Bovary* and Mrs. Morel in D.H. Lawrence's *Sons and Lovers*.

The key word in the assignment is "compare." Comparing two people or objects is a way of defining them. In other words, we learn what one thing is by finding out how it differs from something else.

The tone of the essay is serious, and it is written in a formal style.

- Before you begin, decide on your emphasis. Is your teacher asking you to compare one book that you have been studying in class with another that you have also been studying? If so, you want to emphasize both books. Or are you comparing one familiar work with another that is unfamiliar? In that case, you are probably meant to use the second work to find out more about the first.

- Compare similar things. You won't learn much comparing, say, the structure of one poem with the characterization in another. Start with common ground, and then show how the two subjects diverge.

You may find it helpful to draw a chart listing the criteria you will be using for your comparison. A chart based on the sample essay might look like this:

Similarities	Differences	
	Morel	Bovary
Both are passionate women	Devoted to her children	In love with the idea of love
Both have failed marriages	Enraged by husband's immoral behaviour	Bored by husband's conformity to social norms

- Avoid jumping back and forth too often between the things or ideas you are comparing. Instead, add variety by mixing the order in which you deal with each object or idea you are comparing.

Avoid: Both apples and oranges are colourful and have pleasant textures. Apples are red, yellow, or green. Apples are also crunchy. Oranges are orange. They are also soft.

Acceptable: Both apples and oranges are colourful, but while apples are red, yellow, or green, oranges are orange. And, while both have pleasant textures, oranges tend to be soft, whereas apples are crunchy.

Acceptable: Both apples and oranges are colourful, but while apples are red, oranges are orange. The soft texture of an orange also contrasts with the crunchiness of an apple, although both have pleasant textures.

Now let's look at the structure of the sample essay.

The INTRODUCTION states which characters are being compared and establishes the common ground between the two women. The thesis statement is "They possessed many similar characteristics but were strikingly different in their attitude towards their families."

The BODY consists of four paragraphs, each of which begins with a statement about a similarity or difference between the two characters. The examples given in support of each statement relate back to the thesis statement.

The CONCLUSION summarizes what the comparison revealed.

Shawna Yarnell
English OA1
Mr. Guthrie
November 13, 19XX

Madame Bovary and Mrs. Morel

Mrs. Morel from D.H. Lawrence's novel *Sons and Lovers* and Mme. Bovary from Flaubert's novel *Madame Bovary* were both victims of the restrictions placed on women by society in their respective time periods. These restrictions served to mold their personalities and inevitably determine their tragic destinies. Both women actively attempted to escape from the trials of everyday life and achieve a particular ambition. They possessed many similar characteristics but were strikingly different in their attitude towards their families.

Mme. Bovary and Mrs. Morel were both very passionate women, but each had different ways of expressing her emotions. Mme. Bovary had several tempestuous affairs because her relationship with her husband was unsatisfying to her. In contrast, Mrs. Morel transferred all of the passion she once felt for her husband onto her children. Much of her energy was devoted to raising and educating her sons, who were her only source of happiness. Mme. Bovary took little notice of her daughter except when she was gripped by frenzies of guilt (Flaubert 126). Even then she felt no real attachment and would abandon the little girl for any chance to be with her lovers. Failed marriages were main sources of conflict in both women's lives. Mrs. Morel became so enraged by her husband's immoral behaviour that she would recklessly goad him, often to the point where he became violent (Lawrence 43). She stood her ground and fought so viciously that her husband cowered before her. Mme. Bovary also rebelled against her husband, by refusing to care for herself and being disagreeable to others. She also claimed to approve of immoral things which horrified Charles. She was in love with the idea of being in love. She would often fantasize about the ideal lover and when she was repeatedly disappointed by her lovers, her thoughts turned to death. Both women ended their lives by sacrificing themselves. Mme. Bovary viewed suicide as the only way to free herself from all the pain and misfortune she brought upon herself (Flaubert 372). Mrs. Morel's self-sacrifice was prompted by her belief that the only way for her son Paul to achieve happiness would be through her death (Lawrence 382). The differences in their motivations for suicide illustrate that Mme. Bovary gave much less consideration to her family's well-being that Mrs. Morel did.

Mme. Bovary had a more romantic disposition than Mrs. Morel. Mme. Bovary's main ideas about love and happiness were fostered by the romance novels she read in her youth (Flaubert 43). Her fanciful ideals were first evident in her plans to be married at midnight by torchlight (Flaubert 30). Mrs. Morel, however, is portrayed as a very realistic and reserved woman with little use for sentimental daydreams. Mme. Bovary felt that her boring marriage to Charles was the exception to the rule. She was sure that almost everyone else was happily married. To her credit, she attempted to bring out her husband's romantic side by reciting poetry and singing to him in the moonlight (Flaubert 48). But it was Rudolphe who brought her dreams to life. His velvet cloaks and suede riding boots were right out of the pages of her romance novels. Admittedly, Mrs. Morel also had her romantic side. She kept for many years a Bible which was given to her by a previous admirer as a symbol of their unattainable union, and once revealed that she felt that her son William was a knight who wore her favour in battle (Lawrence 81). Mme. Bovary focused all her romantic daydreams outside her family, for they could not provide her with what her mind and body craved. Mrs. Morel on the other hand was faithful to her husband despite their differences, and instead focused on her children's success.

Clearly Mrs. Morel exhibited the more obvious maternal instincts of the two women. Even though she no longer loved her husband, she never considered leaving her family. Through hard work Mrs. Morel made it possible for her children to be well educated and did everything she could to prepare them for work. She even went to an interview with her son, Paul, to ensure that he got the job (Lawrence 94). Mme. Bovary, on the other hand, was rather indifferent to her daughter most of the time. Once she even lashed out and injured the child in her frustration (Flaubert 136). Mrs. Morel felt her sons were extensions of herself. She was overjoyed at her sons' successes and lived vicariously through them to achieve her own ambitions. Mme. Bovary displayed her maternal qualities in her relationships with her lovers. Rudolphe played on her sympathy by describing the sadness and frustration of his life (Flaubert 163). Madame Bovary later referred to Leon as a "poor boy" and said that she was too old for him (Flaubert 280). She found his youth and timidity highly appealing.

Mrs. Morel and Mme. Bovary were expected to play comparable roles in society. They were wives, mothers, and housekeepers rather than individuals. Their well-being depended on the success and generosity of their husbands, and, bourgeois at heart, each eventually accepted what she believed to be her destiny. Faced with like dilemmas, the two women behaved very differently towards their families. However, many of the same characteristics dominated their personalities, and parallel emotions make the two stories surprisingly similar.

WORKS CITED

Flaubert, Gustave. *Madame Bovary*. New York: W.W. Norton, 1965.

Lawrence, D.H. *Sons and Lovers*. Toronto: Penguin, 1984.

CROSS-REFERENCE

▶ You can see the edited version of the first page of this essay on page 27.

SAMPLE ESSAY #3

Write an essay arguing for or against the idea of cloning human beings.

The key word here is "argue."

The tone of the piece is serious, and it is fairly informal.

When you argue for or against something, you are trying to convince your readers to believe or to do something. Your opinion is right up front. Your success will depend on how well you support your opinion. The more solid facts you can muster, the stronger your argument will be. Read some newspaper editorials for examples of good persuasive arguments. Pay particular attention to your audience and what is likely to convince *them*. Don't be afraid to include opposing arguments. If you are able to counter them effectively, they will only strengthen your case.

TYPES OF ARGUMENTS TO AVOID:

Appeals to majority opinion "Everybody says that cloning is wrong." (Instead, find someone with credibility who disapproves of the idea, e.g., the protests launched by the European countries.)

Leaps of logic "Clones will be treated as less than human and bred for parts." (Just because something could happen, it doesn't necessarily follow that it will. Use "could" or "might" rather than "will.")

Exaggeration "If we allow cloning to continue, the world will end." (Better to say something like, "great risks will be taken if cloning is allowed to continue.")

Vague assertions "Clones could be used in horrifying ways." (Either say nothing, or name ways that they might be used, e.g., as spare parts.)

Now, let's look closely at the sample essay.

The INTRODUCTION grabs our attention with an account of the experiments performed by Dr. Hall. It ends with the strong, startling thesis that "cloning human embryos is completely morally wrong."

The BODY sets forth arguments to prove that it is morally wrong and suggests actions that should be taken. The author has chosen to arrange her ideas from most important to least important. She has used a combination of ideas, examples, and incidents to back up her thesis.

The CONCLUSION summarizes the author's point of view and concludes that cloning must be stopped.

Sue Kim
Journalism
Mrs. Birch
March 19XX

Cloning Express

In October 1993 at the American Fertility Society in Montreal, Jerry Hall reported an extraordinary new experiment. He had accomplished something that science fiction fanatics only ever dreamed about. Using an innovative technique, Hall cloned 17 human embryos into 48. The technique? He waited for the embryo to divide into two, then he stripped the outer coating to separate the two cells, and finally replaced the outer coating with an artificial one. Two embryos with the exact same genetic information were manufactured. Essentially, they were two of the exact same human being. Two humans which could be made into four. Or eight. Or sixteen. The very idea that this could be done is overwhelming—even fascinating. It's tempting to imagine all of the possibilities that Hall's experiment exposes. But like a dark cloud looming over a parade, one thing remains. Cloning human embryos is completely morally wrong.

Hall had used a defective embryo to begin his experiment, in order that the replicated embryos would ultimately be destroyed by nature. Although the embryos died by natural causes and not by an outside force, Hall's experiment is not justified by any means. The fact remains that the possibility of cloning is now open. It is horrifying to think of the ways in which clones could be used. Parents could produce extra embryos of their child to insure that they would have access to perfectly compatible spare parts from the clones for a child who might need it in the future. Or worse yet, clones could be produced for parts, to be sold commercially. A couple could find their ideal child, both physically and in personality, and buy a cloned embryo to raise the exact child.

After the initial horror about human cloning wears off, people may become indifferent to the moral issues involved. When the concept of test-tube babies was first introduced, a lot of people were outraged. How could science oppose nature in such a manipulative way? Now, speaking of test-tube babies will produce not much more of a reaction from people than a yawn. Twenty years from now, after a surge of experimentation with human clones, it's possible that people will feel that same apathy.

Cloning is not new. For years now, scientists have used cloning in crops, mice, and even cattle. But it's impossible to say that experimentation with the cloning of humans would produce the positive results that the cloning of these others have produced. Clearly, we are not the moral equals to crops, rats, or cattle. Researchers cannot simply manipulate potential human beings in the name of science and ignore the moral issues involved. It is arguable that a human clone could be made and live a perfectly productive life. But the temptation to consider these clones as man-made and therefore lesser human beings would not easily be overcome by society, and in considering clones as artificial humans, it would be easy to justify the use of clones for spare parts or labour. The potential result is terrifying.

How can this kind of experimentation be stopped? When the news of Hall's experiment reached the ears of countries like France, Japan, Australia, and people around the world, a flood of protests and outcries were produced. In Germany, cloning of a human embryo is punishable by up to five years in prison. In Britain, the penalty is up to ten years' imprisonment. America too, should realize that cloning is a criminal offence, and there should be punishment within the law. America has many underground markets for drugs, weapons, and stolen goods. Despite the law enforcement, these black markets are always in operation. A law should be established *now* to stop the cloning experiments because if they are allowed to continue, law enforcement will not be able to stop the black market for human clones and clone parts that will inevitably follow.

Human cloning is no longer something to be fascinated by in a science fiction novel. The possibility of producing a human clone is very real and so are the moral issues that follow. If cloning experiments are allowed to continue, the consequences could be frightening. It is our moral responsibility to look at these consequences before they actually happen. In examining the possible outcomes of human cloning experiments, it is obvious that great risks would be taken if cloning is allowed to continue. These are risks we can't afford to take.

CHAPTER 5

WRITING RESEARCH PAPERS

A research paper is similar to a long essay. However, in a research paper the majority of the information you present is drawn from other sources. Your contribution to the thesis lies in which facts and ideas you choose to include, the interpretation you give them, and the way you organize them. In other words, you are using other people's ideas and information to support your own conclusions. The quality of the conclusions and the arrangement of information from various sources to create a single, credible piece of writing is what distinguishes a well-written research paper from a simple factual report.

You will need some special skills to write a research paper. This chapter will show you how to approach a research project systematically and will help you acquire the research skills you will need to find information.

RESEARCH PAPERS

In a research paper, you incorporate your own thoughts with other people's words and thoughts and give credit to those people. Research papers are usually formal in style. Their purpose can be to inform or explain, to present a new point of view, or to present research findings. You will need two special skills to write a good research paper:

1. You have to know how to use the library.

2. You have to know how to document and present your research.

APPLYING THE WRITING PROCESS

Writing a research paper involves the same process as any other writing project, with a few additions. Here is an overview of how to write a research paper, listing the sections in this chapter and elsewhere that can help.

STAGE OF WRITING PROCESS	TIPS AND TECHNIQUES	WHERE TO LOOK
Find and limit your topic	If you are unfamiliar with the subject matter, begin by preparing a preliminary bibliography to help you narrow your topic.	Preliminary Bibliography, page 120
Define your purpose and audience	As always, be clear why you are writing and for whom you are writing.	Define Your Purpose and Audience, page 13
Gather your thoughts	Based on what you learned while preparing your preliminary bibliography, list all that you know about the subject, and then write down questions that you would like to answer. Use your questions to guide your research.	Posing Research Questions, page 122
	Answer the questions by reading and taking notes on the sources listed on your bibliography. Record not only what each source says, but also who said it and where, to avoid plagiarism.	Taking Notes on Cards, page 122 Avoiding Plagiarism, page 133
	Use your list of questions to guide your research, but also let your research guide your questions; you can refine, alter, or redirect your line of inquiry as you find out about the topic.	

STAGE OF WRITING PROCESS	TIPS AND TECHNIQUES	WHERE TO LOOK
Organize your thoughts	Make an outline or tree diagram based on the questions you formulated during your research. Include only information that is relevant to your specific topic, and arrange it in such a way as to express your particular point of view, opinion, or angle on the subject matter.	Organize Your Thoughts, page 13
Write a first draft	As you write, be particularly careful to avoid presenting other people's words or ideas as your own. Even in a first draft, include citations to indicate where you got your information.	Avoiding Plagiarism, page 133 Acknowledging Your Sources, page 125
Revise for focus, content, and structure		Revising, page 22
Edit paragraphs, sentences, and words	Do not change the words in a direct quotation.	Editing, page 25 Quotations in an Essay, page 79
Proofread and format the final draft	Make sure you have acknowledged all of your sources correctly, and finalize any figures or graphs you may want to include. Add front and back matter, including a list of works cited and/or a bibliography.	Acknowledging Your Sources, page 125 Visual Aids, page 85

USING THE LIBRARY

Most libraries contain the following materials:

1. books in circulation
2. reference materials
3. magazines and newspapers
4. audiovisual materials
5. special resources

Books in Circulation

Most books in the library are in circulation, meaning that you can take them out. Books cover just about any topic you can think of, but the information they contain is not always up-to-date. Most information in books is at least a year old. Also, remember that the broader the area a book covers, the less detailed the information will probably be. A book on Canadian geography won't tell you as much about the Rockies as will a book on the Rockies. Be selective. Still, books are often the best resource for a research paper because there are so many of them, and they cover so many topics.

WHERE TO FIND THE BOOK YOU WANT: THE MAIN CATALOGUE

Most libraries have a computerized catalogue listing all the books (reference books as well as those in circulation) in the library's collection. You can use the computer to search by author, title, or subject. The same book will usually have a listing under each of these files. For example, if you are looking up information on American rock singers, you could look in the subject catalogue under *rock music— singers—United States*. If you are looking for a specific book called *The Death of Elvis* you would look in the title catalogue under that title. If you are not sure of the title, but know that one of the authors' names was Charles C. Thompson II, you could look in the author catalogue under *Thompson, Charles C.*

Here is a sample entry for a book called *The Death of Elvis*.

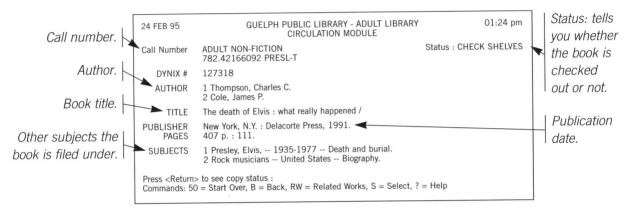

Many computerized catalogues also allow you to search using subject or title key words. If you cannot find what you are looking for using the author, title, or subject, try these more general search techniques.

Once you find what you want in the catalogue, write down the call number. This tells you where to find the book in the stacks. Fiction books are arranged alphabetically by author. Non-fiction books are arranged on the shelves according to subject area. Each subject area has a number from 000 to 900 assigned to it. For example, books on Fine Arts (painting, sculpture, music, etc.) are each given a call number from 700 to 799. In this catalogue, *The Death of Elvis* has the call number 782.42166092 PRESL-T.

Reference Materials

Reference materials give factual information, free from opinion. They are a great source of background and summary material. As well, some reference sources tell you where to find information. On the other hand, printed reference materials don't usually provide the most up-to-date data. Also, you can't take them out of the library.

The following pages list some useful reference books that might be available at your library.

Word or Phrase Dictionaries

Some large dictionaries include a great deal of information that you would normally expect to find in an encyclopedia.

There are also dictionaries for particular fields, such as law and medicine, and for certain subjects, such as mythology.

Gage Canadian Dictionary A good guide to Canadian spelling and to some specifically Canadian words.

The Oxford English Dictionary This thirteen-volume dictionary follows British spelling and pronunciation, which is similar to what we use in Canada.

Biographical Dictionaries

Dictionary of Current Biography

Macmillan Dictionary of Canadian Biography

Who's Who
There are *Who's Who* books for international, Canadian, British, and American figures.

General Encyclopedias

Encyclopedias are a great place to start if you want a short summary of a particular topic.

The Canadian Encyclopedia

The Junior Encyclopedia of Canada

Collier's Encyclopedia

World Book Encyclopedia

Almanacs and Yearbooks

Almanacs are yearly calendars that contain statistical information of various kinds. Yearbooks may contain a chronicle of the events that take place in a given year, arranged by subject. Or they may focus on one particular subject area, such as the arts, astronomy, or politics.

The World Almanac and Book of Facts

The Canadian World Almanac and Book of Facts

The People's Almanac

Facts on File

Canadian News Facts

Atlases and Gazetteers

An atlas contains maps. A gazetteer gives brief historical information about various places along with a pronunciation guide to place names.

Oxford Canadian Atlas of the World

Historical Atlas of Canada

Columbia Lippincott Gazetteer of the World

Webster's Geographical Dictionary (a gazetteer)

Quotations

Need a catchy quotation to get your essay going? Try one of the following, browse through the section in your library, or check out the subject index of *Books in Print* (under *quotations*).

Bartlett's Familiar Quotations

The Oxford Dictionary of Quotations

Colombo's Canadian Quotations

The Oxford Dictionary of Modern Quotations

Indexes

An index is a list of resources available for a particular topic. There are indexes to cover all sorts of topics and interests.

Books in Print
These volumes list all the books that are published in the United States (as well as Canadian books that are sold in the U.S.), and are updated each year. You can search for books by author, title, subject, or publisher. There is also an index titled *Canadian Books in Print. Whittaker's Books in Print* lists books published in the U.K.

Canadian Periodical Index
A subject listing of articles from most Canadian (and some American) magazines and journals.

Readers' Guide to Periodical Literature
A subject listing of articles from most American, and some Canadian, magazines.

Canadian News Index
A subject list of articles from major Canadian newspapers.

History References

These references and others like them give an overview of different historical periods.

Cambridge Ancient History

Cambridge History of the British Empire

Cambridge Medieval History

Literature and Drama References

Literary History of Canada

The Oxford Companion to Canadian History and Literature

The Oxford Companion to English Literature

The Oxford Companion to the Theatre

The Readers' Encyclopedia

Philosophy and Mythology References

A Handbook of Greek Mythology

Larousse World Mythology

The Encyclopedia of Philosophy

Music and Art References

Encyclopedia of World Art

Grove's Dictionary of Music and Musicians

The New Oxford History of Music

Science and Technology References

Applied Science and Technology Index

A Dictionary of Geology

The Encyclopedia of the Biological Sciences

The Environment Index

The Gaia Atlas of Planet Management

McGraw-Hill Encyclopedia of Science and Technology

APPLY IT!

▶ *Go to your local library and find at least one of the references in each of the categories in the list above. Record the call number in your notebook, and refer to it the next time you need information in one of those subject areas.*

CROSS-REFERENCE

▶ To find out how to use the main catalogue, see page 112.

WHERE TO FIND REFERENCE MATERIALS
Libraries may store reference materials in a special reference section, on CD-ROM database, or on microfilm. Reference books are kept together in a separate section, arranged by call number. They are usually listed in the main catalogue along with other books. For the location of reference materials on CD-ROM or microfilm, ask your librarian.

Magazines and Newspapers

Articles can give you more up-to-date information than most books can, but keep in mind that many articles combine facts with the opinions of the writer. Don't mistake one for the other.

Most libraries do not lend out current copies of magazines and news-papers. However, some will allow you to check out older magazines. Find out what the rules are at your library.

WHERE TO FIND MAGAZINE AND NEWSPAPER ARTICLES

Magazines are often called periodicals. Newspapers are sometimes included under this term as well. The first place to look for articles is in a periodicals index. The most useful of these are the *Readers' Guide to Periodical Literature* (covering most American and some Canadian magazines) and the *Canadian Periodicals Index*. Some libraries have these indexes on a CD-ROM database. Otherwise, you will find them in the reference section. (Check the catalogue or ask the reference libra-rian.) The indexes are arranged by topic, and each current volume con-tains the titles of all the articles written on the topic in a given month. At the end of the year, the volumes are compiled into a single hard-cover book. If you don't find anything on your topic in the most current book, look in the volumes that cover previous months.

> It is much easier to search for articles on a database, so be sure to find out if your library has a periodicals index on computer.

Bear in mind that not all periodicals listed in these indexes will be available in your local library. Most libraries have a periodicals desk with a list of what is available. To get a magazine, you usually fill out a form at the desk listing the specific edition you want, including the title, month, year, and volume number, if there is one. Then the librar-ian gets it for you. Current newspapers are often stored on racks or shelves. Back issues may be kept with the magazines at the periodi-cals desk or stored on microfilm and kept in a special filing cabinet.

> Your greatest resource in a library is the reference librarian. Reference librarians spend their days answering questions and help-ing people to find what they need. They love to help! Use them!

USING MICROFILM

Microfilm is a way of storing newspapers, magazines, and other docu-ments on film. Usually, each reel contains about two weeks' worth of newspapers. To view a magazine or newspaper on microfilm, ask for the reel that contains the date you are interested in, and thread the film onto a microfilm viewer. Get the librarian to show you how. Some machines allow you to take photocopies of one page at a time. On other machines, you will have to read the article on screen and take notes.

▶ *Create a chart to record the periodicals available at your local library. Make columns for the title of the periodical, the dates available, whether or not it's on microfilm, and other notes (such as location, whether it can be checked out, etc.) that may be useful to you in later research. Check your library for the following key resources:* The Globe and Mail, Maclean's, Canadian Geographic, Report on Business, The Financial Times, Omni, Equinox, *and* Saturday Night.

Special Resources

Every library has special resources. You will have to learn what is available at your own library, but here are some possibilities.

1. AN INFORMATION FILE

This is a filing cabinet or box containing pamphlets, generally arranged alphabetically by subject. These pamphlets may be issued by government departments, companies, professional groups, universities, or individual concerns.

2. A VERTICAL FILE

This is a filing cabinet containing pictures and clippings from newspapers and magazines. They are usually arranged alphabetically by subject.

3. AUDIOVISUAL MATERIALS

Most libraries have videos that you can borrow. They may not be first run, but they are free! Some also have compact disks, cassettes, films, and multimedia kits. Sometimes these resources are listed in a separate catalogue; other times they are included in the main library catalogue.

Can't find the book you want at your local library? Most libraries can order a book from another library system on *interlibrary loan*. It may take a while for the book to arrive, though, so make the request as soon as possible. Also, if the book comes from some private or university libraries, there may be a fee. Ask in advance.

4. DATABASES

A database is a collection of information on a particular subject. More and more libraries are acquiring databases on CD-ROM (compact disk read-only memory), which allow users to search for information in a particular field by computer. Looking for information using a CD-ROM database is quicker and more efficient than searching through printed indexes or reference books because all the entries are cross-referenced, and the database includes information for several years, rather than just one.

> A CD-ROM can store the equivalent of 275 000 pages of information. That's a lot of shelf space!

There are two types of databases. *Reference databases* tell you where to find information on a particular topic. They may list books or other printed materials on the subject, or they may tell you about organizations or individuals that can help. *Source databases* provide the information itself; some contain statistics and surveys, while others contain complete dictionaries, encyclopedias, or newspaper or magazine articles, for example. The indexes listed on page 114 may be available on CD-ROM. Here are some databases that may be available at your local library.

Reference Databases

Canadian Business and Current Affairs (CBCA)
A compilation of four indexes (including the *Canadian News Index* and the *Canadian Magazine Index*). Emphasizes business stories.

General Periodical Index
Lists 1100 general interest business and academic publications. Includes some Canadian sources.

Bowker's Complete Video Directory
Lists over 62 000 videos.

Source Databases

Oxford English Dictionary

Compton's MultiMedia Encyclopedia

New Encyclopedia Brittanica

> Be sure to find out what is available on computer database before you begin your library search. It can save you a lot of time.

A P P L Y I T !

▶ *Prepare a list of all databases available at your local library. Keep it in your notebook to give you a head start when doing research.*

BEYOND THE LIBRARY: OTHER RESOURCES

You will probably do most or all of your research at the library. However, if you can't find what you need there, consider using one or more of these other sources.

CROSS-REFERENCE

▶ See page 194 for tips on conducting interviews.

1. PEOPLE IN THE COMMUNITY

Most people are happy to grant you a short interview if they have information that can help you. Interviews are useful when you are writing newspaper articles and some essays. But be sure your sources are trustworthy, and try to corroborate facts they tell you through another source (articles, books, or other interviews).

2. RADIO AND TELEVISION

Watch for programs related to your topic. Take notes and write down the program, the name of the producer, and the date, time, and station on which the program was shown so you can credit your source.

3. GOVERNMENT DEPARTMENTS

The federal government has a toll-free number that offers information and referral to federal programs and services. This is a good place to start if you are trying to get information from the government but do not know what department to call. In most of Canada, the toll-free number is 1–800–667–3355. In Quebec and Manitoba, check in the blue pages of your phone book under Reference Canada.

Once you have figured out what department to contact, call or write to the "Public Relations Department" there.

Statistics Canada is the government department that collects statistics about Canada and Canadians. All data from the Census (a survey of all Canadians taken every ten years) is tabulated by Statistics Canada. If you want up-to-date statistics on some aspect of Canadian society, phone their toll-free line at 1-800-263-1136.

4. COMMUNITY AGENCIES

The Chamber of Commerce can give you information on your local community: businesses, tourism, population, etc. Look in the phone book for your area.

Other local businesses and public service organizations may also be able to provide you with specific information on issues of concern to your local community. For example, if you are writing a paper or article about food banks, consider interviewing the local food bank director or at least reading over any pamphlets they have that explain their services.

5. COMPUTER NETWORKS

If your computer is hooked up to the Internet or another computer network, you have access to all sorts of useful information. Here is a rundown of the main functions of networks that are of interest to researchers:

- *Electronic mail*
  Using e-mail, you can talk to any other computer on the network. Try writing to the premier of your province, or to your local MP,

asking his or her opinion on a particular issue. Or, join an e-mail list and join in group conversations.

- *Information retrieval*
  Some examples of information files available on the Internet include library catalogues, company files, Supreme Court decisions, and stock exchange information.

- *Bulletin boards*
  There is a bulletin board out there for just about any topic you care to name. If you are looking for information or ideas that are not readily available in a library, try posting a query on a bulletin board. You will almost certainly get several answers. While bulletin boards are a quick way to get an answer to a question, be sure to corroborate information you receive from anonymous sources. In other words, try to find a documented source (book, article, quotation from a recognized authority, etc.) that backs up the information you find on a bulletin board.

PREPARING A PRELIMINARY BIBLIOGRAPHY

A preliminary bibliography is a list of all the books, magazines, newspapers, and special resources that contain material related to your topic. Preparing a preliminary bibliography on a general topic will familiarize you with

- the general subject area,
- what resources are available on the subject, and
- what specific aspects of the subject interest you.

If you need to narrow down a broad subject, preparing a preliminary bibliography is a good idea.

Let's say your assignment is as follows:

Research and write a paper on an issue related to managing our water supply.

1. Begin by making a cluster or list based on the key word "water." This will give you some ideas to help guide your library research.

2. Then go to the main computer catalogue and do a subject search under "water." If there are too many books listed under that heading, narrow it further using some of your key words. For example, you might look under "water supply" or "fresh water" or "water conservation." Remember, though, that you want to gather more sources in your bibliography than you will actually use in your paper.

3. For each card in the catalogue that looks like it might be interesting or useful, make your own 7 cm x 13 cm (3" x 5") file card, one card per book or resource. Copy the information from the catalogue exactly. These cards are your preliminary bibliography.

> If you are writing a research paper that is due in, say, four weeks, plan to spend about a day narrowing down your topic.

Cossi, Olga   *Call No.: 333.91 COS*

Water Wars: The Fight to Control and Conserve Nature's Most Precious Resource

Don Mills, Ontario: Maxwell MacMillan Canada, 1993.

---

4. Survey each resource you have listed on your cards. Find the book and spend a few minutes finding out if it is of any use to you.

   • Check the table of contents, the date of publication, and the index.

   • Scan the potentially relevant sections.

   • Note on your card whether the information is general or detailed or accompanied by charts, graphs, maps, or other illustrations.

5. Ask yourself two questions:

   • What areas are well covered in the resource materials I have surveyed?

   • Which of the areas that are covered are both significant and interesting?

Now you can go through your cards and set aside those books not related to your narrowed down area of interest.

> Do not throw away the unused cards from your bibliography. A few of them might come in handy later on. *Do* make sure that you set them aside, away from the cards you want to use right away, though.

POSING RESEARCH QUESTIONS

Once you have skimmed through the books in your preliminary bibliography and narrowed down your area of interest, prepare a chart like the one below, based on the information you have picked up so far.

Topic	What I Know	What I Don't Know
Water Scarcity	- World's fresh water supplies are dwindling	- What are the main causes of the shortage?
	- Lack of clean, drinkable water is a major cause of disease in some countries	- Where is it scarce?
		- What are the other consequences of the scarcity?
		- How can we manage the water supply more efficiently?
	- Canada has one of the largest supplies of fresh water in the world.	- How are supplies distributed around the world?
		- Can they be redistributed?

Now, use the questions listed in the last column to guide your research. You may even want to create a new chart, using each point of information in column 2 as a topic heading in column 1.

Topic	What I Know	What I Don't Know
Scarcity of Fresh Water	Main reasons for drop in supply is population growth and increased industrial uses of water.	What can be done to manage the water supply?

In this way, you can gather and organize your information and change or refine your questions as you go.

TAKING NOTES

Now you need to gather more information to answer your questions. This means taking notes, using the resources on your preliminary bibliography. Choose one of the following methods, or invent your own. Be sure, though, to keep careful track of where you got your ideas, and whether they are paraphrases or direct quotations. Otherwise you may end up inadvertently plagiarizing (stealing ideas or expressions).

CROSS-REFERENCE

▶ For general tips on how to take good notes, see page 211. For how to avoid plagiarism, see *Avoiding Plagiarism*, page 133.

METHOD 1: *Taking Notes on Cards*

If the paper you are planning is long, complicated, or if you will be using a lot of resources, try using file cards to organize your note taking. Here is how to do it:

1. Read the relevant parts of each resource.

2. Put the author's name and the title (in a shortened form) in the upper left-hand corner of each card you make.

3. Put one, and only one, piece of information or quotation on each card. Include the page number where you found the information.

4. Leave the top right-hand corner blank, or write a few key words in pencil to indicate which of your research questions the card relates to. Later, you can replace these key words with words related to your rough outline.

5. Try to take notes in your own words, rather than just listing quotations. Doing so will help you to think about what you are reading.

6. If you find a passage that you think would make a good quotation, copy it down *exactly*, and enclose it in quotation marks.

7. You can also make idea cards as you read. Idea cards can contain your own observations about, and interpretations of, the material you have read.

Author and title (shortened form).

Subject relative to your research questions.

Information written in your own words (put direct quotations in quotation marks).

Page where you found the information.

> Postel, *Last Oasis* → Reasons for Scarcity
>
> Although water does replenish itself, it does so at a rate determined by nature, not by the needs of a growing population.
> p. 28

METHOD 2: *Taking Notes in Chart Form*

If you are writing a shorter research paper, you may want to write your notes in a list or chart. Down the left-hand column, write headings based on your main research questions. Across the top, put each of the sources from your preliminary bibliography.

	Water Wars	To the Last Drop	World Resources
Causes of Shortage	- uneven distribution (23)	etc...	etc...
	- population growth (23)		
Distribution of Fresh Water			

ORGANIZING YOUR INFORMATION

Since research papers tend to be fairly long and complex, it is usually a good idea to write some kind of an outline based on your notes before you start writing. Use your research questions to help you create main heads and subheads. If you use cards, you can spread them out on the floor or on a large surface, and rearrange them under appropriate headings or themes.

TOPIC: MANAGING OUR WATER SUPPLIES

I. WHY WE NEED TO MANAGE THE WATER SUPPLY

    A. Distribution of world's fresh water and sources of fresh water

    B. Increasing demand for fresh water

       1. Industry

       2. Population growth

    C. Diminishing supplies of fresh water

II. THREATS TO FRESH WATER SUPPLIES

    A. Pollution

    B. Wasteful agricultural practices

    C. Greenhouse effect

    D. Exploitation of non-renewable water sources

III. SOLUTIONS

    A. Stop big engineering projects

    B. Use less wasteful irrigation methods

    C. Change consumer practices

ACKNOWLEDGING YOUR SOURCES

As you write a research paper, be sure to give credit to your sources. There are several ways to do this. One of the most popular is the MLA (Modern Languages Association) style of in-text citations. However, some teachers may prefer you to use footnotes or endnotes. You will find guidelines for both methods in this section.

In-text Citations

Include a citation in the following cases:

1. When you are expressing someone else's idea (paraphrase).

2. When you are quoting someone directly.

3. When someone might question your accuracy (for example, if you have used statistics).

The only cases in which you do not need a citation are when you are expressing your own ideas or when the information is common knowledge (dates of well-known events, for example).

A citation should include only as much information as a reader needs to look up the full source information in the reference list at the end of the paper. In the case of most books or articles, this means the author's name and the page number.

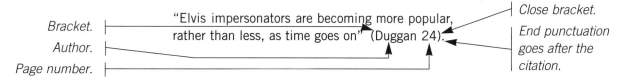

If you mention the author's name in the phrase leading up to the quotation, you don't need to include that information in the brackets:

> According to Duggan, "Elvis impersonators are becoming more popular, rather than less, as time goes on" (24).

Here is the proper format for MLA in-text citations:

Two or more authors or editors Include both names in every citation, either in the text or in the parentheses.

> James and Lanthier found that most Elvis impersonators were extremely insecure when not performing their Elvis act (3).

> Many Elvis impersonators are extremely insecure when not performing their act (James and Lanthier 3).

Three or more authors or editors In the first citation, include all the names. Any time after that, you can just write the first name followed by "and others."

According to Wolfgang, Figlio, and Sellin, most crimes are committed by relatively few hardcore offenders.... It is also true that most disadvantaged people are law-abiding citizens (Wolfgang and others 45).

Two authors with the same last name or two different works by the same author
Use the title of the work to differentiate authors with the same name or different works by the same author. The other alternative is to name the work in the body of your essay.

Passion is characteristic of the Brontes' characters. This passage is typical: "Gentle reader, may you never feel what I then felt! May your eyes never shed such stormy, scalding, heart-wrung tears as poured from mine" (*Jane Eyre* 365).

Passion is characteristic of the Brontes' characters. This passage from Charlotte's *Jane Eyre* is typical: "Gentle reader, may you never feel what I then felt! May your eyes never shed such stormy, scalding, heart-wrung tears as poured from mine" (365).

A corporate or government author Use the full name of the department or organization, unless there is a very well-known abbreviation.

(Statistics Canada)

(UNESCO 7)

No author given If you don't know the author, identify the source using the title or part of the title. (Set it in italics, or underline it if you are writing by hand or on a typewriter.) For example, an entry from page 224 of the *Dictionary of Canadian Biography* would be cited as follows:

(*Dictionary* 224)

A work with several volumes Make clear which volume of a work you are referring to (if you use more than one volume) by adding the volume number in the parentheses. If you are citing a page number, put the volume number first, followed by a colon and the page number.

(*Groves* 2: 224)

Citing two or more works If you want to cite two or more works together, separate the two citations by a semicolon.

(Gardner 66; Lasch 124)

CHECKLIST FOR IN-TEXT CITATIONS

Have I:

☑ Included an in-text citation and a reference for all paraphrases, direct quotations, and statistics or diagrams taken from another source?

☑ Identified the author's name (if known) and the page number, either in the text or in parentheses, for each citation?

☑ Avoided repeating in the parentheses information already mentioned in the text?

☑ Copied the names of authors exactly from the original source?

☑ Separated each in-text citation within the same parentheses with a semicolon?

Footnotes
Footnotes go at the bottom of the page. If you prefer, you can collect all your footnotes together and write them in a numbered list at the end of your paper. These are called endnotes. The only thing you need to put in the body of the text is a superscript (above the line) number. This is how a footnote looks at the bottom of a page:

Quotation within the paper.

Footnote number raised slightly above the line.

Line separating footnote from the rest of the paper.

Footnote.

"North Americans in particular have adopted ice cream as a food central to their mythology, a symbol almost of national identity."[1]

- -

[1]Margaret Visser, *Much Depends on Dinner* (Toronto: McClelland & Stewart, 1989), 373.

Here is an overview of the format to use for footnotes.

• Indent all footnotes on the first line and single space them.

• Begin most footnotes with the author's name (first name first).

• Next, give the title. Titles of articles or chapters go in quotation marks. Use italics or underlining for book or magazine titles.

• Put the publication information next, in parentheses: the place of publication, the publisher's name, and the date the book was published.

• Write the exact page number(s) where the material was found.

• Once you have referenced a source in a footnote, all following references to the same source can be shorter.

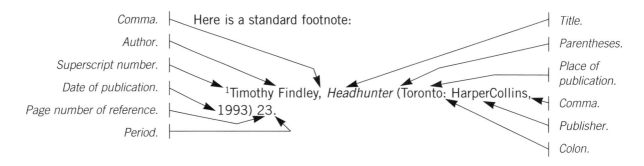

Here is a series of examples, showing how to footnote different kinds of sources.

1. SOURCES USED FOR THE FIRST TIME

Single author or editor

[1]Margaret Visser, *Much Depends on Dinner* (Toronto: McClelland & Stewart, 1989) 373.

Two authors or editors

[2]Douglas Bowie and Tom Shoebridge (eds.), *Best Canadian Screenplays* (Kingston: Quarry Press, 1992) 23–26.

No author given

[3]*The New Canadian Oxford Atlas* (Toronto: Oxford University Press, 1977) 44.

A work with several volumes

[4]Maurice Horn, ed., *The World Encyclopedia of Cartoons*, vol. 2 (New York: Chelsea House, 1981) 33.

Work in an anthology

[5]Ruth Rosen, "Soap Operas," *Watching Television*, ed. Todd Gitlin (New York: Pantheon, 1986) 42.

Translation

[6]Roch Carrier, *La Guerre, Yes Sir!*, trans. Sheila Fischman (Toronto: House of Anansi Press, 1970) 145.

Magazine or encyclopedia article

[7]Zachary Margulis, "Canada's Thought Police" *Wired* March 1995: 92.

Corporate author

[8]Ministry of Industry, Trade and Commerce, *Canada Handbook 1994* (Ottawa: Supply and Services Canada, 1995) 43.

Newspaper article

[9]Charna Bagatan, "Native Leaders Make Strong Demands," *The Globe and Mail* 10 Mar. 1996: D3.

Videos and movies

[10]*Lismer*, Dir. Allan Wargon (National Film Board of Canada, Canadian Artists Series, 1952).

Recording

[11]Guiseppe Verdi, *Arias*, New Philharmonia Orchestra, Simon Estes, bass and Gaetano Delogu, cond. (Philips, 416 818–4, 1987).

Interview

[12]Harlo Wilson, personal interview, January 27, 1995.

CD ROM

[13]Victor Rosenberg, "Computers," *The New Grolier Electronic Encyclopedia* (Danbury, CT: Grolier Electronic Publishing, Inc., 1988), CD-ROM.

2. SOURCES USED MORE THAN ONCE

If you have already footnoted a source, you can use a shortened footnote for later references:

[14]Bagatan 90.

If you are using two or more books by the same author, or if two authors you are using have the same last name, include the title, or part of it.

[15]Takami. *Handbook* 90.

> Besides acknowledging sources, you can also use footnotes to add extra information that doesn't really belong in the body of your paper: additional research findings, background information, or definitions of terms, for example. Keep these kinds of footnotes to a minimum.

CHECKLIST FOR FOOTNOTES

Have I:

☑ Included a footnote or endnote for all paraphrased ideas, direct quotations, and statistics or diagrams taken from another source?

☑ Included all the necessary information in each footnote?

☑ Used correct punctuation?

☑ Separated two sources cited in the same note with a semicolon?

☑ Numbered each reference in the text consecutively with a super-script number?

☑ Placed each footnote at the bottom of the page on which the reference appears, separated from the text by a line, indented, and beginning with a superscript number?

☑ Placed endnotes following the last page of the paper, in a numbered (not superscript) list?

List of Works Cited or Bibliography

If you use in-text citations, you also need to include a list of all the works cited in your paper. If you use footnotes, you need to add a bibliography at the end of the paper. In either case, the format for entries is the same, except that the entries in a list of works cited are double-spaced. Here is a sample of a basic reference for a book.

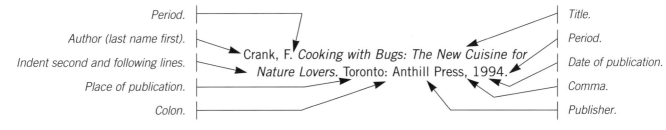

Period.
Author (last name first).
Indent second and following lines.
Place of publication.
Colon.

Crank, F. *Cooking with Bugs: The New Cuisine for Nature Lovers.* Toronto: Anthill Press, 1994.

Title.
Period.
Date of publication.
Comma.
Publisher.

> There is a slight but important difference between a list of works cited and a bibliography. The former lists all the works you actually cite in your paper while the latter lists all the works you consulted, whether you actually refer to them or not. If you read sources that you never actually cited, but that did relate to your topic, you may want to include *both* a list of works cited *and* a bibliography.

• Start the first line of each entry at the left-hand margin. If the entry runs more than one line, indent all lines after the first.

• Arrange the list alphabetically by author. For sources with no author, use the title of the book (*The*, *An*, or *A* don't count).

• Put the author's last name first. Include all of the authors if there is more than one.

• Next, include the title, the place of publication, the publisher's name, and the date it was published. You will find all this information on the copyright page of the book.

Here are some sample entries for a reference list:

Single author
Aaronson, Sylvia. *A History of Cash Registers*. Toronto: Moneytalks Press, 1995.

Several authors
Brown, Tom, Richard Smith, and Harry Jones. *Unusual Names*. London: Whittaker, 1989.

Editors
Chu, Sandra and Mark Pick, eds. *Decision Making Models*. New York: Wall Street Press, 1995.

Unknown author
The Chicago Manual of Style. 13th ed. Chicago: University of Chicago Press, 1982.

Author and editor
Donne, John. *Selected Poems*. Ed. Sally Forth. San Francisco: Southern University Press, 1994.

Encyclopedia
Wilson, J. Tuzo. "Plate Tectonics." *The Canadian Encyclopedia*. 1988 ed.

Translation
Dostoyevski, Fyodor. *The Idiot*. Trans. David Magarshack. Harmondsworth: Penguin, 1982.

Corporate author
Ontario Human Rights Commission. *Human Rights: Employment Application Forms and Interviews*. Toronto: OHRC, 1991.

Work in an anthology
Forster, E.M. "The Machine Stops." *Classics of Modern Fiction: Ten Short Novels*. Ed. Irving Howe. New York: Harcourt Brace Jovanovich, 1972.

Magazine article
Picovich, Edward. "School of the Future: Plugged in Learning." *Maclean's* 30 Sept. 1991: 25–32.

Newspaper article
DeLonghi, Greta. "Project Haiti's Hospital Sees a Sunny Future." *Guelph Tribune* 19 October 1994: 12.

"Ottawa Plans Major Cutbacks." *The Globe and Mail* 20 Feb. 1992: A1.

Videos, television shows, and movies

The Big Snit. Dir. Richard Condie. National Film Board of Canada, 1985.

Recording

Verdi, Guiseppe. *Arias.* Simon Estes, Bass. Cond. Gaetano Delogu. New Philharmonia Orchestra. Philips, 416 818–4, 1987.

Interview

Springsteen, Bruce. Personal interview. 15 Oct. 1995.

CD-ROM

DISCovering Authors, Canadian Edition. Vers. 1.0. Biographical database. On CD-ROM. IBM. Detroit: Gale Research, 1994.

CHECKLIST FOR WORKS CITED OR BIBLIOGRAPHY

Have I:

- ☑ Included a reference for every footnote, endnote, or in-text citation?
- ☑ Begun each entry at the left margin and indented all following lines?
- ☑ Arranged the list alphabetically by author?
- ☑ Checked the punctuation and capitalization?
- ☑ Rechecked the information against the original source to make sure it is correct?

Ask your teacher what form of documentation he or she prefers. Don't mix methods!

Abbreviations Used in Footnotes and Bibliographies

anon.	anonymous
col.	column
cols.	columns
comp.	compiled
ed.	editor or edition
eds.	editors or editions
et al.	(Latin *et alia*) and others
Ibid.	(Latin *ibidem*) in the same place
n.d.	no date
p.	page
pp.	pages
rev.	revision or revised
rpt.	reprint

trans.	translated by
vol.	volume
vols.	volumes

AVOIDING PLAGIARISM

Plagiarism is using someone else's words or ideas as if they were your own. Not only is plagiarism unfair to the writers you steal from, it is illegal.

To avoid plagiarism:

1. Cite a source for any phrases or ideas that are not completely your own.

2. Reword and rephrase borrowed material.

3. Put any direct quotations in quotation marks and credit the source.

An example of original source material:

> The United Nations estimated that the provision of potable water could cut the world's infant mortality rate in half and in 1980 the world organization announced the decade of clean water and sanitation. But the goal of clean water for all by 1990 failed to grab the headlines the way starvation in Africa has and there has been little support for the waterworks.
>
> From Michael Keating (environment writer, Toronto), *To the Last Drop: Canada and the World's Water Crisis.* (Toronto: MacMillan of Canada, 1986), 112–113.

Plagiarized: Although the United Nations estimated that the provision of potable water could cut the world's infant mortality rate by 50 percent, the decade of clean water and sanitation that ended in 1990 failed to grab the headlines. There has been little support for poor nations in need of such help.

Even if this passage cited a source, it would still be suspect, since the author has borrowed whole phrases from the original source without using quotation marks. Two acceptable alternatives are illustrated below. The first uses direct quotation marks and a citation. The second paraphrases the original without quotation marks and cites the source.

Acceptable: In 1980, the United Nations declared the start of its decade of clean water and sanitation. With better water supplies, it claimed, the global infant mortality rate could be reduced by 50 percent. However, according to Keating, "the goal of clean water for all by 1990 failed to grab the headlines," and there was "little support" for poor nations in need of basic water and sanitation facilities (112–113).

Acceptable: The United Nations' declaration in 1980 of the decade of clean water and sanitation had little impact, in spite of the UN's claim that the infant mortality rate could be reduced by 50 percent if clean water were made more available (Keating 112–113).

It is easy when you are starting out to misrepresent ideas as your own without meaning to. To avoid falling into this trap, you need to be aware of the issue throughout the process of writing your research paper. Here is an overview of how you can avoid plagiarism as you follow the writing process:

- Take the time to write notes in your own words, and avoid borrowing phrases from the original source. Writing in your own words will not only help you avoid plagiarism later, it will force you to work through the material as you go.

- Write down a source for *all ideas that are not your own.*

- When you do write down a direct quotation in your notes, be sure to include quotation marks to remind yourself that these are not your own words.

- Include citations in the first draft of your paper; do not leave them until the end and try to insert them after the fact.

- Double check your *Works Cited* or *Bibliography* entries against the original sources to make sure they are accurate.

T R Y I T !

I. Rewrite each of the following passages to avoid plagiarism. Rephrase passages, insert quotation marks, and add in-text citations as necessary.

Original Source:
The biggest of all the big arguments in language circles over the last thirty years has been over how each of us learns to talk: is our language ability innate, inborn, or do we learn language from scratch the same way we learn so much of our other behaviour? Linguist Noam Chomsky, who claims it's innate, has so dominated this field since the late fifties that while normally you'd describe a debate like this as having two sides, his and the other's, somehow in this case it seems that Chomsky is at the centre, with all other points of view swirling around him. Even those who agree with him that much or all of our language ability is innate still stake out their own slightly different piece of territory.

From *Talk, Talk, Talk* by Jay Ingram. Copyright © Jay Ingram, 1992. Reprinted by permission of Penguin Books Canada Limited.

Passage:
Since the 1960s, one of the most controversial areas of linguistics has been the question of how we learn language. Linguist Noam Chomsky has been at the centre of the debate for decades. His view,

that we are born with the ability to learn language, has so dominated this field since the late fifties that while normally you'd describe a debate like this as having two sides, his and the other's, somehow in this case it seems that Chomsky is at the centre, with all other points of view swirling around him.

Original Source Material:
Ever since white settlers stumbled upon these stone rings 110 years ago, medicine wheels have generated as much controversy as misunderstanding. Made of sun-bleached boulders that range from the size of human heads to buffalo skulls, each stone structure has a unique shape; many, like Onoka-Katzi, don't even look like wheels. The 150 surviving medicine wheels of North America are mostly located in southern Alberta and Saskatchewan, with a smaller number in Montana and Wyoming. Although their exact purpose remains the subject of intriguing theories among archeologists, Plains Indians have never forgotten their reason for being. They served various purposes, such as commemorating the dead, frightening away enemies such as the Cree, and anchoring spiritual observances such as communion with the Blackfoot creator and the spirits of the land.

From Andrew Nikiforuk, "Sacred Circles" *Canadian Geographic* July/August 1992: 51. Reprinted with permission of the author.

Passage:
There are 150 medicine wheels still intact in North America, mostly located in southern Alberta and Saskatchewan. Montana and Wyoming also have some examples. The wheels were used for different purposes, such as commemorating the dead, frightening away enemies, and anchoring spiritual observances (Nikiforuk 51).

2. *Paraphrase the following material without plagiarizing it. Do not quote more than one or two sentences directly, and be sure to use quotation marks, citations, and paraphrasing as necessary.*

For decades, scientists have known that southwestern British Columbia is the most active earthquake region in Canada, shaken by more than 300 earthquakes annually. Most tremors are too small to be felt or have occurred in unpopulated areas, although history records a structurally damaging earthquake about every 25 to 45 years. Now, however, Canadian and American scientists are convinced that at least six or seven giant earthquakes have ruptured the region in the last 7000 years, and they believe that the Pacific Northwest could be heading toward one of the most severe earthquakes in recorded history.

From Anne Tempelman-Kluit, "Countdown to Cataclysm," *Best Canadian Essays 1990* (Saskatoon: Fifth House, 1990), 78. Essay first published in *Equinox* September/October 1989.

PRESENTING A RESEARCH PAPER

Once you have finished writing your paper, and have prepared a reference list, you need to present it in a suitable format. The chart of the writing process in Chapter 1 provides some tips under the heading *Presenting*. If your paper includes several headings, you will need to prepare a table of contents. If you have used several figures, include a table of figures as well. Here is a list of all the elements possible in a research paper, in the proper order. (Use a new page for each element.)

1. Title page
2. Table of Contents
3. Table of Figures
4. Essay
5. Appendices
6. Works Cited
7. Bibliography

> **CROSS-REFERENCE**
>
> ▶ For samples of these elements, see Chapter 3, beginning on page 88.

Visual Aids

Visual aids, such as figures, graphs, charts, maps, and diagrams, can be very useful in a research paper. For example, maps can be very useful if you are discussing a particular area of the world. Timelines can help in history research papers to remind your readers of how the events you are discussing relate to each other and to other historical events.

On the other hand, visual aids aren't necessary in all research papers. Don't use them to pad an essay: your reader (i.e., your teacher) won't be fooled!

> **CROSS-REFERENCE**
>
> ▶ For general information on how to use figures and graphs, see page 85.

BUSINESS AND TECHNICAL WRITING

▶ *A*t some time, all of us have to communicate in writing with businesses or the government, be it to complain about faulty merchandise, request information, or apply for a job. There is a correct way to do all of these things. The advice in this chapter will help you write effective business letters, job applications, résumés, and memos. It also provides guidelines for, and samples of, a variety of reports and tips on conveying technical information to a non-technical audience.

CONTENTS

APPLYING THE WRITING PROCESS

When you write business letters, memos, and reports, follow the writing process model presented in Chapter 1. Pay particular attention to two aspects of the process:

- identify your audience and focus on their level of expertise, and
- organize your writing so that the most important information is easy to find.

STAGE OF WRITING PROCESS	TIPS AND TECHNIQUES	WHERE TO LOOK
Find and limit your topic	In business writing, your topic is usually predetermined by the situation.	Find and Limit Your Topic, page 11
Define your purpose and audience	It is crucial in business writing to know exactly who your audience is, how much they know about your subject, and what you want them to know about it. Be sure you consider not only the primary reader of your work, but also any secondary readers who may be given a copy. You may have to include some extra information for their benefit.	Define Your Purpose and Audience, page 13 The Business Reader, page 139
Gather your thoughts		Gather Your Thoughts, page 13
Organize your thoughts	In business writing, always put the most important information right up front. The rest of the writing fills in the details.	Organize Your Thoughts, page 13
Write a first draft	Find the right balance between conciseness and completeness in the information you choose to include in your writing. In other words, tell your audience what they need to know to understand what you are telling them, but do not waste their time with unnecessary details.	The Structure of Business Writing, page 139
Revise for focus, content, and structure		Revising, page 22
Edit paragraphs, sentences, and words		Editing, page 25
Proofread and format the final draft	The format of your work will depend on the type of document you have written and its degree of formality. Consult the samples in each specific section in this chapter for more information.	

THE BUSINESS READER

No matter what kind of business writing you are preparing, your audience is likely to include business executives or managers. Your work may also be read by technical experts or staff members who are delegated to deal with the issue presented. Here are some characteristics of business readers to keep in mind as you write.

- They want the facts, presented in a clear, concise, and easy-to-understand format.

- They will probably require some background information, since the topic under consideration is likely just one of many they are dealing with.

- They are often interested in the bottom line: costs, schedules, revenues, etc.

- They need to be able to find the most important information easily.

THE STRUCTURE OF BUSINESS WRITING

The Beginning

Whatever you are writing, your first paragraph should tell your reader what you most want him or her to know. This approach is quite different from the introduction you would write for an essay or research paper. Do not waste your reader's time with background information at this point. One way to make sure you come right to the point is to begin with the words "I want to tell you that...." Later, you can cross out these words and use what is left as your introduction.

(I want to tell you that...) The furnace at 75 Wooster Rd., Unit 45, exploded on Monday. There was extensive damage to the basement, but there were no personal injuries to the inhabitants. We need to replace the furnace, and repair the damage to the structure as soon as possible.

The Body

The body of your writing fills in the necessary background and details. Never include unnecessary information in a business document, but be sure your audience has all the information necessary to act.

The Ending

Business documents do not usually conclude the way essays or research papers do. How you end a business document will vary depending on your specific purpose in writing. Your ending may

summarize the contents of the communication,

recommend a course of action,

make a specific request, or

present qualifications.

> Whoever your audience is for business or technical communication, you can be sure that he or she is extremely busy. Always get right to the point.

BUSINESS LETTERS

Business letters can be used to make requests, place orders for goods, check on orders already placed, make claims for damages, explain your views, or express thanks (for example, to a guest speaker or for an interview). You can write a letter to a friend any way you feel like writing it and on any kind of paper, but business letters need extra attention.

- Be formal, clear, concise, and make sure to include all the information the recipient needs to know about the matter at hand.

- Write business letters on standard 21.5 cm x 28.0 cm (8 1/2" x 11") white paper. If possible, use a computer. (Many copy shops have computers that you can use for a small hourly fee.) If you *must* write by hand, be neat!

- Pay careful attention to grammar, spelling, and punctuation.

You can apply the writing process described in Chapter 1 to business letters. Pay particular attention to defining your purpose and identifying your audience. Be clear about what your goal is in writing.

The examples that follow show some suggested formats for business letters.

Requesting Information

Purpose: To find out more about my ancestors from the archives of the Canadian Jewish Congress.

Audience: Director of Archives at the Congress.

The following sample letter illustrates the pattern of all business letters:

- It is addressed to a specific person. Whenever possible, try to get a name before you write to a large organization.

- The first paragraph comes to the point right away, summarizing exactly why the writer is writing.

- The tone of the letter is formal and polite, but neither flattering nor apologetic.

- The second-to-last paragraph defines the action being requested, so that the recipient knows exactly what it is the writer wants her to do.

- The last paragraph contains a sentence of "thanks in advance" and notes that a self-addressed stamped envelope is enclosed.

- Some other acceptable closings for business letters are
  Yours very truly,
  Yours sincerely,
  Yours faithfully,
  Yours respectfully,

- If the letter had been typed by someone other than Simon Frank, the typist would have put his or her own initials in lowercase, followed by a slash, and then Simon's initials in capital letters: el/SF. This shorthand information would be included a few lines below the signature, just before "enclosure."

Writer's address.

1700 Elm Street
Willowdale, Ontario
M3C 6P3

Date.

August 21, 19XX

Name and address of recipient at left margin.

Janice Rosen
Director of Archives, Canadian Jewish Congress
1590 Ave. Docteur Penfield
Montreal, Quebec
H3G 1C5

Salutation followed by colon.

Dear Ms. Rosen:

my point right-a-way —

Each paragraph begins at left margin with no indent.

I recently started tracing my family tree and have found that one of my great-great-uncles settled in Quebec. The Jewish Genealogical Society suggested that I write to you as a possible source of information. *experience*

Single-spaced except between paragraphs; one line space between paragraphs.

My great-great-uncle's name was Samuel Joseph Schwartz. He was born in Cambridge, Massachusetts (date unknown) and died in Montreal on August 24, 1945. His father's name was William A. Schwartz, and his mother's name was Annie Sheaffer.

Tell what want

Closing followed by comma.

I would appreciate any help you could give me, either regarding my uncle or regarding other sources of information. If there is a fee involved, please let me know in advance.

Space for signature.

THANKS in advance

Thank you for your help. I have enclosed a self-addressed, stamped envelope for your reply.

Full name of sender—you may include Mr., Mrs., Miss, or Ms. in parentheses.

Yours sincerely,

Simon Frank

Simon Frank

Indicates that some other material (i.e., an envelope) accompanies the letter.

enclosure

▶ *Write a letter to a university or community college you are interested in attending, requesting information about admission requirements, course offerings, and anything else you want to know. Use the format and tips given above in drafting and presenting your letter.*

Complaint

Purpose: To exchange a sweater.

Audience: Sales manager of T. Eaton Co.

---

7 Rue Landry
Ste Justine-de-Dorchester, Quebec
H4T 1R8

November 20, 19XX

Mr. Timothy Eaton
T. Eaton Co. Ltd.
Rue Ste Catherine
Montreal, Quebec
H3H 5T6

Dear Mr. Eaton:

I am returning the hockey sweater you sent me on November 16 for an exchange or refund. Not only does it have the wrong team logo, but, as you can see, it fell apart after only one wearing.

On November 1, I ordered a Montreal Canadiens hockey sweater for my son through your Fall and Winter catalogue (item no. 402 067 32Y A, p. 247). The sweater that arrived two weeks later had the Toronto Maple Leafs logo. Although my son was very disappointed, I was willing to overlook the mistake and keep the sweater.

My son wore it once to play hockey, and the next day the material had disintegrated almost completely. You would think to look at it that a swarm of hungry moths had devoured it whole. However, nothing else in the drawer has been damaged, and I cannot imagine any moths, no matter how hungry, eating through a whole sweater so quickly. We have never had this trouble with the Canadiens sweaters you have sent us in the past. Clearly, the sweater was of very poor quality.

Please send a Montreal Canadiens sweater as quickly as possible. If you do not have any in stock, please refund my money. Kindly do not send another Maple Leafs sweater.

Thank you for your swift attention to this matter. My son looks forward to receiving his new sweater.

Yours truly,

Marie Carrier

Marie Carrier

Letter to an Editor or Member of Parliament

Purpose: To express my views regarding the no-skateboarding bylaw passed by City Council.

Audience: The general public and members of City Council.

If you disagree with something that is happening in your community, or would like to express your opinion about a political issue, you may want to write to your local paper or to your member of parliament.

7 Simpson St.
Milborne, Saskatchewan
S4P 5T3

May 8, 19XX

Editor
Milborne Sentinel
14 Main Street
Milborne, Saskatchewan
S8R 2P8

Dear Sir or Madam:

I am writing to express my disagreement with the decision of city council to outlaw skateboarding in Saint Patrick's Square (see "City Council Bans Skateboards" *Sentinel*, May 7, 19XX, p. A4).

This decision is unfair to young people. Wouldn't city councillors rather see us engaged in a healthy and entertaining sport than hanging around in malls or wandering the streets with nothing to do? There are not many places for young people to spend their time downtown. Take away our skateboarding, and there will be even fewer.

If safety is the councillors' main concern, why not simply pass a bylaw that skateboarders have to wear proper protective gear? No one I know would object to that, since we all wear pads and helmets anyway.

Or is the real purpose of the bylaw to get young people out of the square altogether?

I urge the councillors to reconsider their decision and the public to let their support for skateboarding be known.

Yours truly,

Philippa Lao

Philippa Lao

Here are some things to remember when writing a letter of this type:

- If you are responding to a news article, cite the headline, newspaper, date, and page number. If you are writing to a Member of Parliament or other official, describe the situation you are referring to, and make sure that you are writing to the appropriate representative (municipal, provincial, or federal).

- State your views firmly but politely, and back them up with reasons, facts, and logical arguments. You may make an emotional appeal as well, but don't let emotions substitute for hard facts.

- If it is appropriate, suggest possible solutions or actions that you think your readers should take.

- Make a copy of the letter and keep it for reference.

A P P L Y   I T !

▶ *Read your local newspaper and familiarize yourself with an issue that concerns you. Then write a letter to the editor of the paper expressing your view on the subject.*

Long Business Letters If your letter takes up more than one page, write "continues" in the bottom right-hand corner of each page except the last. At the top left-hand corner of each page (except the first) write the name of the person or company the letter is addressed to, the page number, and the date.

T. Eaton Co.
Page 2
19XX-11-2

Continues

Sending Letters ENVELOPES AND FOLDING

- Use a standard white business size envelope measuring 24 cm x 10.5 cm (9 1/2" x 4 1/8").

- Include your return address in the top left corner, as well as the complete address of the person to whom you are writing. Here is how the envelope should look:

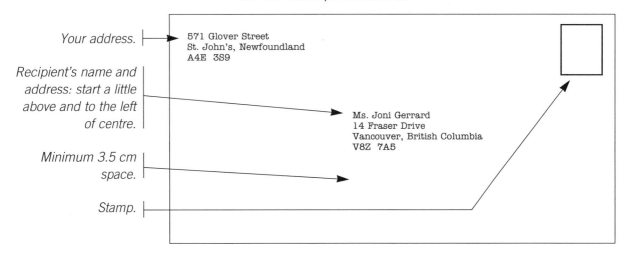

Your address.

571 Glover Street
St. John's, Newfoundland
A4E 3S9

Recipient's name and address: start a little above and to the left of centre.

Ms. Joni Gerrard
14 Fraser Drive
Vancouver, British Columbia
V8Z 7A5

Minimum 3.5 cm space.

Stamp.

- Fold business letters in thirds. Remember to include any extra material, such as a résumé.

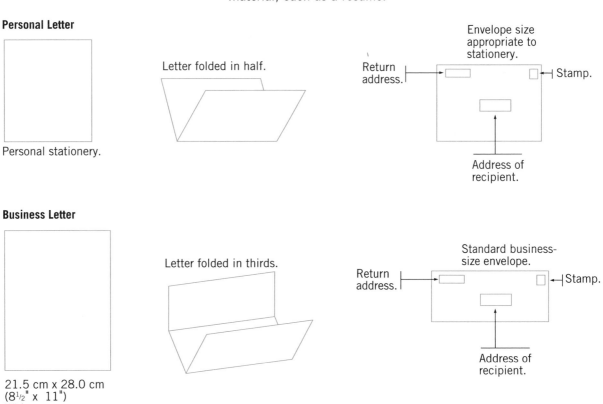

Personal Letter

Personal stationery.

Letter folded in half.

Envelope size appropriate to stationery.

Return address.

Stamp.

Address of recipient.

Business Letter

21.5 cm x 28.0 cm
(8½" x 11")
White paper.

Letter folded in thirds.

Standard business-size envelope.

Return address.

Stamp.

Address of recipient.

- Before mailing your letter, double check the envelope. Is the address complete and correct (including the postal code)? Have you remembered to put on a stamp?

SENDING FAX TRANSMISSIONS

When sending a letter or document by fax, be sure to include the following information, either at the top of the first page or on a separate cover sheet:

- the name, title, company, and fax number of the receiver;

- your name and address (If you are writing on behalf of a company, include your title. Include the company name only if this is not included on the letterhead.);

- your phone number;

- the total number of pages in the transmission, including the cover sheet;

- the date.

Follow the model below when sending letters by fax.

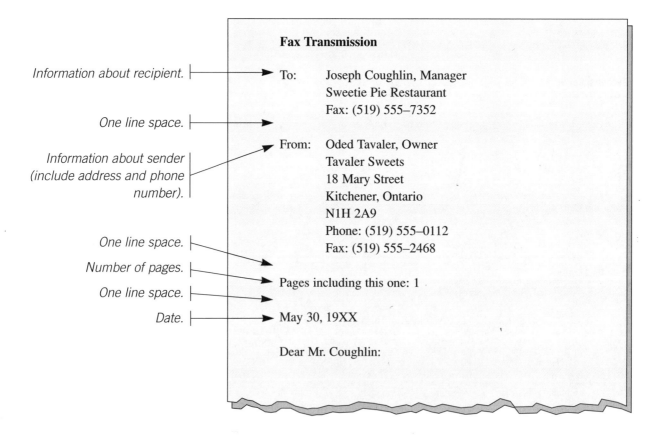

Information about recipient.

One line space.

Information about sender (include address and phone number).

One line space.

Number of pages.

One line space.

Date.

Fax Transmission

To: Joseph Coughlin, Manager
         Sweetie Pie Restaurant
         Fax: (519) 555–7352

From: Oded Tavaler, Owner
         Tavaler Sweets
         18 Mary Street
         Kitchener, Ontario
         N1H 2A9
         Phone: (519) 555–0112
         Fax: (519) 555–2468

Pages including this one: 1

May 30, 19XX

Dear Mr. Coughlin:

CHECKLIST FOR LETTER WRITING

Have I:

☑ Composed my message with my purpose and audience clearly in mind?

☑ Stated my reason for writing in the first paragraph, and ended the letter with a clear request for any action I want my reader to take?

☑ Included background information that will be useful and relevant to my reader?

☑ Written formally and politely, without apologizing?

☑ Followed the formats for business letters given in this section?

☑ Proofread my letter for spelling, grammar, and punctuation errors?

☑ Kept a copy of the letter for reference?

☑ Signed the letter and attached any enclosures?

☑ Addressed and stamped the envelope or prepared a fax transmission sheet?

LETTERS SEEKING EMPLOYMENT

You will need to write two kinds of letters when you are applying for jobs. The first is a letter of application, which accompanies your résumé when you first apply. The second is a letter of thanks after you have been interviewed. In both cases, you need to be extremely careful to make a good impression. Pay particular attention to details of spelling, grammar, punctuation, and proper format. *Always* write employment letters on a computer or typewriter.

> Consider spending a little extra to have your résumé and letter of application laser printed on high quality paper. Stick to conservative colours, like white, off-white, cream, or grey paper.

Job Application

Purpose: To apply and be favourably considered for a job advertised in the newspaper.

Audience: Ms. Vera Shimano, Personnel Manager.

A letter of application should fit on one page. You can adapt the pattern of the sample letter that follows to fit almost any job application.

15 Scargill Ave.
Vancouver, B.C.
V2A 2T7

May 2, 19XX

Ms. Vera Shimano
Personnel Director, Rent-a-Clown Enterprises
27 Robson St., Suite 17
Vancouver, B.C.
V5C 2B8

Dear Ms. Shimano:

I am writing to apply for the position of clown at Rent-a-Clown Enterprises, as advertised in the *Vancouver Sun* on April 29.

Last year, I took part in a workshop on clowning and street theatre given at our school. This experience gave me a strong interest in clowning, which I am eager to pursue. Since September, I have been a volunteer at the Children's Hospital, entertaining sick children once a week as KoKo the Clown.

For the last four years, I have been actively involved in the drama club at Cartwright High School, from which I will graduate in June of this year. Last year, I was president of the club. As well as performing in every major play the club has staged in the last four years, I have worked on lighting, makeup, props, and other aspects of production. I especially enjoyed acting in our 1994 year-end comedy revue. My one-person mime skit won the prize for best performance of the evening.

My résumé, which is enclosed, shows that I have spent the last two summers working as a camp counsellor at Camp Oranoak. This experience taught me leadership skills, including how to keep young children interested and entertained. In addition, I know how to perform magic tricks and can make animals out of balloons.

I would very much like to meet with you to learn more about the position at Rent-a-Clown and discuss my qualifications. I will call you next week to find out when it would be convenient for us to get together.

Yours sincerely,

Maya Lefkowitz

(Ms.) Maya Lefkowitz (alias KoKo the Clown)

enclosure

Each paragraph performs a specific function:

1. The first paragraph identifies the purpose of the letter and the specific job you are applying for.

2. The following paragraphs call attention to your qualifications, highlighting areas that apply to the specific job, and mention that a résumé (and any other supplementary information) is enclosed.

3. The last paragraph expresses enthusiasm for the job and the company and a desire to be granted an interview.

> Unless you have been specifically told not to phone, end your letter by promising to make a follow-up call. If you just say, "I look forward to hearing from you," you may have a long wait!

Follow-up

Purpose: To follow up on my job interview.

Audience: Ms. Shimano, Personnel Director.

Goal: I am writing a brief, formal letter as a follow-up to the job interview I had with Ms. Shimano.

The purpose of this type of letter is to keep your name fresh in the potential employer's mind. Such a letter shows courtesy, initiative, and persistence.

The pattern for follow-up letters is straightforward:

- Paragraph 1 thanks the interviewer for granting you the interview and mentions the job in question specifically.

- Paragraph 2 notes something specific you learned in the interview and tells why this piece of information was interesting and exciting to you. Use this paragraph to remind the interviewer that you are well-qualified for the job.

- Paragraph 3 restates your enthusiasm for the job and the company.

15 Scargill Ave.
Vancouver, B.C.
V2A 2T7

May 12, 1994

Ms. Vera Shimano
Personnel Director, Rent-a-Clown Enterprises
27 Robson St., Suite 17
Vancouver, B.C.
V5C 2B8

Dear Ms. Shimano:

Thank you for taking the time to discuss the summer position at Rent-a-Clown yesterday. It was both entertaining and enlightening to learn about the challenges and rewards of working as a children's entertainer.

I was particularly interested to hear that you provide ongoing workshops for your clowns. As I mentioned during the interview, I am always interested in learning new clowning skills, and I love working with young children.

I know that I could be an asset to your firm and would like the opportunity to prove it to you. Again, thank you for considering my application. I look forward to hearing from you and possibly working with you in the near future.

Yours sincerely,

Maya Lefkowitz

(Ms.) Maya Lefkowitz (alias KoKo the Clown)

Résumés Most employers will want to see your résumé before they hire you. A résumé should present a profile of your experience from an employer's point of view. Here are the categories to cover, usually in this order:

1. Personal Data Your name, address, and phone number are essential.

> DO NOT include your date of birth, marital status, race, religion, a photograph, or any other information that does not relate directly to your ability to do the job. It is also advisable not to include your social insurance number until the job is actually offered to you.

2. Education Give the name of the school you attend and list any courses, seminars, or workshops you are taking or have taken that relate directly to the kind of job you are seeking. Be sure to call attention to any awards or outstanding scholastic achievements.

3. Work Experience Include any full-time, part-time, or summer jobs you have had, as well as volunteer work.

4. Activities and Interests Use this section to tell your potential employers about any hidden talents you have. List important skills you have not mentioned elsewhere, any special activities you have participated in, and hobbies or interests that reflect well on you. The information in this section can also be used to show that you have a sense of responsibility, a talent for leadership, or a well-rounded personality, all of which will help you get a job.

5. References Choose two or three people who know you well enough to speak knowledgeably and fairly about you. Former employers make the best job references. After former employers, consider teachers, school staff, neighbours, and friends' parents—in that order—as potential references. Do not use family members as references, unless you have only ever worked for your Uncle Louis. *Always ask permission before putting someone's name down as a reference.*

> Instead of listing names, you may simply state, "References available upon request," and bring the references with you on a separate sheet of paper when you go to the interview.

Try to get all this information on one sheet of paper, but use two if the résumé is going to look cramped. Always send a covering letter with a résumé, even if you have already spoken with the employer in person or by phone.

Maya Lefkowitz
15 Scargill Ave.
Vancouver, B.C.
V2A 2T7
Phone: (604) 555–2223

EDUCATION

Sept. 1990–Present   Cartwright High School, Vancouver, B.C.
     Will graduate in June of this year. Maintained a B average in first three years. Took drama as an elective in all three years, and received A's consistently each year.

June 1993   Workshop: Be a Clown!
     Participated in a workshop for drama students given by clowns Robert Asch and Marisa Mundt at Cartwright High School.

WORK EXPERIENCE

Volunteer Clown   Vancouver Children's Hospital, Vancouver, B.C. V3R 2A6
         Sept. 1993–Present
     Work as a clown once a week, entertaining sick children on wards at the hospital.

Sales Assistant   Darrah's Florists, 133 Elgin Ave., Vancouver, B.C. V6B 1B7
         Part time, Sept. 1992–May 1993, Sept. 1993–Present
     Serve customers, create flower arrangements, and take orders over the phone at a busy downtown florist shop.

Camp Counsellor   Camp Oranoak, Carswell, B.C. V8A 2C6
         June–August 1992 and June–August 1993
     Supervised children aged 7–9 in a variety of activities, including swimming, hiking, and crafts. Organized, acted in, and directed the "Oranoak Revue," a talent show featuring campers and counsellors. Promoted from Junior Counsellor to Senior Counsellor.

OTHER SKILLS AND INTERESTS

Member of Cartwright High Drama Club, Sept. 1991–Present. Acted as President from Sept. to June 1993.

Completed Red Cross first aid course May, 1992.

REFERENCES

Ms. Pauline Jessamyn, Director, Camp Oranoak, 17 Doxton Cres., Vancouver, B.C. V6T 9B9, (604) 555–3422

Mr. Frederick Warner, Volunteer Coordinator, Vancouver Children's Hospital, Vancouver, B.C. V5H 3F4, (604) 555–6766

CHECKLIST FOR SEEKING EMPLOYMENT

Have I:

☑ Written a complete résumé and made enough copies of it?

☑ Received permission to use the names of two or three people as references?

☑ Written a letter of application?

☑ Prepared to answer questions of a potential employer in an interview?

☑ Written a follow-up letter for each interview granted to me?

CROSS-REFERENCE

▶ For sample questions and tips on how to prepare for an interview, see page 194.

APPLY IT!

▶ *Prepare a résumé and cover letter to apply for a job that interests you. Use one of the following job advertisements, find one in the classified ads in your local paper, or visit a student employment centre.*

1. Wanted
   Part-time helper for small painting company. Suitable for students. Painting experience preferred, but will train the right candidate. Part-time to June, full-time in the summer. Must be willing to work hard. Send résumé to Gail Harper, 233 Ajax Street, Edmonton T2W 1A9.

2. Camp counsellor, live-in, at a prestigious outdoor camp in a beautiful setting. May to August. Applicants must be 16 years of age or older. Lifesaving certificate and camp experience required. Experience working with children an asset. Responsible for supervising activities of campers, aged 6–12. Send or fax résumé by March 15 to Jocelyn Kee, Camp Director, Camp Kichihaha, P.O. Box 269, Station C, Toronto, M4C 1X8, fax (416) 555–3343.

3. Wanted
   Caring young people to work with autistic children. No experience required. Part time, two or three evenings a week. Involves working one on one with an autistic child using a variety of games and activities, under the direction of a program supervisor. Looking for a fulfilling part-time job? This could be it. Send résumé to Karl Froshen, Supervisor, Autistic Stimulation Program, Institute for Child Studies, 224 Brown's Road, Halifax, Nova Scotia.

4. Auto parts supplier requires stock room worker. Must be familiar with auto assembly. Neat appearance. Full-time or part-time. Contact Phillip Ho, Parts Manager, Toronto Toyota, 456 Brant Street, Toronto, Ont. M4C 2X4.

MEMOS

Memos are the main form of communication between members of the same large business or organization. They are also used as a formal record of what goes on in the business. Some companies still send memos on paper, through an inter-office mail system. Others rely on electronic mail (e-mail), which allows employees to send memos directly from their own computer screen to those of any or all of their co-workers.

Memos may convey information, persuade, make requests, or respond to other memos.

Purpose: To remind and inform members about the trip to the Tapp Gallery.

Audience: Members of the photography club.

Memos usually begin with the following headings:
To:
From:
Subject:
Date:

> You will sometimes see "Re" used instead of "Subject." It is an abbreviation for the word *regarding*, which means *about* or *concerning.*

You may want to "copy" a memo to individuals who are not being directly addressed in the letter itself, but who should receive a copy for reference or information. Include these names on a separate line before the subject, under the heading "c" or "copy."

When you write memos, be sure to identify your purpose and your audience. Here are some other points to remember:

- Be accurate. Memos provide a written record of your actions, so it is important that the information you provide is correct. Check dates and schedules, and choose your words carefully to avoid sending unclear messages.

- Be brief. Don't include unnecessary information.

- If more than one person will receive the memo, list the recipients in rank order, from highest to lowest. For example, if the memo is addressed to your manager, your co-worker, and the vice-president, list the vice-president first, your manager second, and your co-worker third.

- Cover one subject only per memo. If you have two issues to discuss, write two memos. Remember, a memo is a written record. It's difficult to file a memo that contains information on two separate subjects.

- In the final paragraph always explain exactly what action (if any) you expect the recipient to take.

- Sign or initial the memo either at the bottom of the page, or next to your typed name at the top. You don't need to include a salutation or a closing.

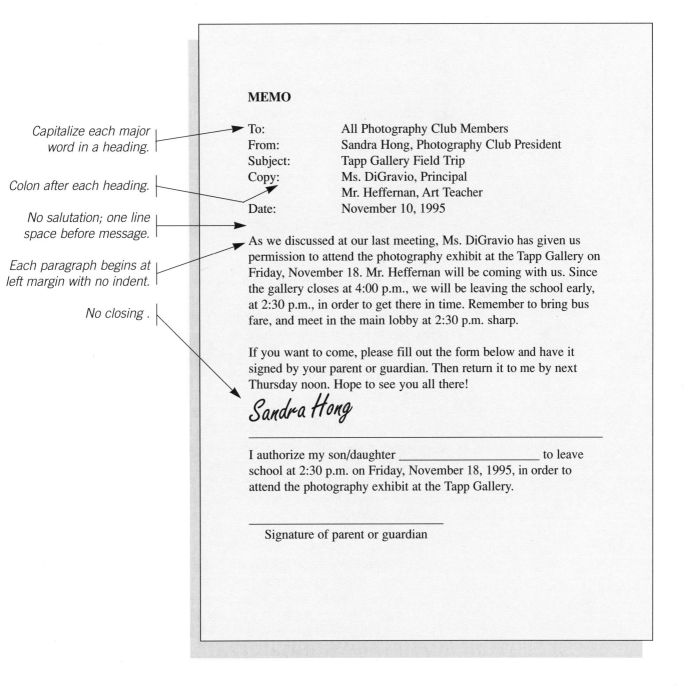

Capitalize each major word in a heading.

Colon after each heading.

No salutation; one line space before message.

Each paragraph begins at left margin with no indent.

No closing .

MEMO

To: All Photography Club Members
From: Sandra Hong, Photography Club President
Subject: Tapp Gallery Field Trip
Copy: Ms. DiGravio, Principal
            Mr. Heffernan, Art Teacher
Date: November 10, 1995

As we discussed at our last meeting, Ms. DiGravio has given us permission to attend the photography exhibit at the Tapp Gallery on Friday, November 18. Mr. Heffernan will be coming with us. Since the gallery closes at 4:00 p.m., we will be leaving the school early, at 2:30 p.m., in order to get there in time. Remember to bring bus fare, and meet in the main lobby at 2:30 p.m. sharp.

If you want to come, please fill out the form below and have it signed by your parent or guardian. Then return it to me by next Thursday noon. Hope to see you all there!

Sandra Hong

I authorize my son/daughter _____ to leave school at 2:30 p.m. on Friday, November 18, 1995, in order to attend the photography exhibit at the Tapp Gallery.

_____
Signature of parent or guardian

CHECKLIST FOR MEMO WRITING

Have I:

☑ Kept my purpose and audience clearly in mind?

☑ Stated my purpose in the first paragraph and explained any actions I want my readers to take at the end of the memo?

☑ Provided accurate and relevant information?

☑ Covered only one subject per memo?

☑ Listed the recipients of the memo in rank order?

☑ Followed the format for memos described in this chapter?

☑ Proofread the memo for grammatical, spelling, or punctuation errors?

☑ Signed or initialled the memo at the bottom of the page or next to my typed name at the top?

REPORTS

A report is a written, systematic statement of facts prepared for a specific purpose and aimed at a specific audience. Knowing how to write reports is useful in business, where you may be asked to prepare a report explaining a new process or product or analyzing the competition.

Here are some report-writing tips to help you at various stages of the writing process.

1. The main purpose of a report is to inform, analyze, or persuade. Examples of reports that inform are progress reports. Evaluation reports analyze a situation, present alternatives, and recommend a course of action, while proposals are usually designed to persuade the reader to adopt a specific course of action. You will find examples of each of these types of reports later in this chapter.

2. Readers of a report are usually busy managers or executives, who commission reports to help them make decisions about specific problems or situations they do not have time to investigate themselves. The report may also be read by technical experts or department heads who will be required to implement the changes.

3. Information for business reports can come from various sources. Try the following to get you started:

   • Company files and publications. Examples include annual

reports, mission statements, informational brochures, job descriptions, and financial records.

- Interviews with employees, suppliers, technicians, etc.

- Observation and experimentation. Personal observations are admissible in informal reports. However, for more formal presentations try to back up your observations using at least one other source. For example, you could back up your observation that there is not enough room in the cafeteria at lunchtime by monitoring cafeteria use over a period of several days, or by conducting a survey.

- Library research. Not all reports require library research. However, you may find useful information in recent business articles and periodicals. Chapter 5 contains more detailed information on how to use the library to do research.

> You may want to consult the Canadian Business and Current Affairs (CBCA) Index for articles on your topic. The index is often available on CD-ROM.

4. As with other forms of business writing, put the most important information up front. The body of the report fills in the details that support the main ideas. In longer or more technical reports, the actual data that support the details may be gathered at the end in appendices and references, or it may be inserted into the body of the report in tables and charts.

> Although reports are usually organized from most important to least important, feel free to arrange individual sections within the report chronologically, by feature, or in any other way that makes sense.

CROSS-REFERENCE

▶ For examples of formal and informal writing, see page 19.

5. Always write a report in a formal style.

6. Be as objective as possible, even when making recommendations. Being objective means letting the facts speak for themselves, presenting both sides of an issue, giving options, and avoiding exaggerations and emotional appeals.

> "Objective" does not have to mean stuffy, wordy, or long-winded. Avoid overusing the passive voice, redundancies, and clichés when writing reports.

7. Unless your report is very short and informal, use headings to identify its various parts. Begin with the functional heading "Introduction," and end with "Summary," for information reports, or "Conclusions" and "Recommendations" for evaluations or proposals. However, try to use more descriptive headings for the detailed discussion in-between. For example, instead of "Background," a report evaluating the usefulness of CD-ROM technology might have headings such as "How CD-ROM Technology Works" or "Current Uses of CD-ROM Technology."

8. Acknowledge your sources. Use the in-text citation method outlined in Chapter 5. Doing so is a legal requirement, and it also lends credibility to your report.

CROSS-REFERENCE

▶ See page 125 for more on in-text citations.

> Informal reports are sometimes presented as memos or letters. To decide how to present your report, check other reports in the company files. Ask your manager or supervisor where to find them.

Progress Reports

Progress reports are often used in businesses to inform management of the status of a particular project. Employees often write progress reports to let their managers know how closely a project is staying on schedule or on budget.

Here are the main parts of a progress report:

1. The introduction highlights the most important information found in the body of the report. Identify the project, work completed, the present situation, and work still to be done. Be sure to highlight any problems that have arisen, and state whether or not the project is on schedule.

2. Begin the body of the report with an overview of the work that has already been completed. The amount of detail you include will depend on how much your reader knows or needs to know. Even when your audience is very involved in the project and is familiar with what has happened, you should include a brief synopsis to remind them.

3. Next, describe the present situation. Describe what is being done and by whom, as well as reporting any delays or problems and how they are being dealt with. End the section by stating when you expect the present phase to be completed.

4. The following section covers work still to be done. Anticipate any problems that might arise, and predict when you think the project will be completed.

5. The summary is optional in a progress report. If you wish, end with a brief overview of the situation as it stands, and a look at what lies ahead.

CROSS-REFERENCE

▶ You will find guidelines for making and placing figures and charts in papers and reports on page 85.

Charts can be very useful for summarizing schedule changes. Try writing specific tasks or phases to be completed down the left-hand column, followed by columns headed Scheduled Completion Date, and Actual Completion Date.

Charbridge Construction
RR 3, Carforth, Alberta T6R 1V3
Phone: (403) 555–8643
Fax: (403) 555–2212

To: James Charbridge, President
From: Bob Shaftoe, Supervisor
Subject: Construction Project, 18 Joseph Avenue
Date: July 24, 19XX
No. of Pages: 2 (including this one)

Introduction

This is in regard to your request for an update regarding the project at 18 Joseph Avenue. The discovery of a lack of foundation in part of the existing house has necessitated changes in plan and construction. The accompanying cost increases will be borne by the client. The completion date will be moved ahead to November 15, a delay of two weeks.

Background

The project at 18 Joseph Avenue involves building an addition onto an existing home, which is approximately 120 years old. The owner of the property, Mr. Miles Matsumoto, had been acting as general contractor until about two weeks ago, when excavation revealed significant design and construction problems. At that point, Charbridge Construction was called in to take over. The project is now being completed under my supervision.

Work Completed

The excavation for a new foundation is complete. It was during the excavation that it was discovered that there was no frost wall underneath the summer kitchen (see Appendix A, attached). Concrete had been poured around the base of the walls, in a good imitation of a foundation wall. At this point, we were contracted to manage the project.

Work Underway

After we were called in, I went to examine the excavation myself, along with Mr. Matsumoto. We decided that the summer kitchen should be demolished and entirely rebuilt, requiring substantial changes to the existing plans. New plans are presently being drawn up. Mr. Matsumoto has agreed to assume the additional costs that will be incurred. Changes required to accommodate the new plans include the following:

- New frost walls to support side wall of new kitchen addition (there will be a crawl space).
- Concrete bench to support foundation of main house.
- The second floor joists will be cantilever over the new kitchen. Truss joists will be used to meet span requirements.

Work Remaining

We expect the new plans tomorrow (July 25). Work on the foundation will resume Saturday, and by Tuesday, framing will begin. I anticipate no further major delays, but the original schedule will have to be revised by approximately two weeks, giving a completion date of November 15, 19XX.

Summary

Although the lack of a foundation was a major setback, the rest of the construction on Joseph Avenue should be fairly routine. Once the new plans have been approved, the construction schedule will resume its normal course. It is even possible that we could make up some of the time lost, if the weather holds during framing.

A P P L Y I T !

Write an informal progress report for a project you are currently working on for one of your classes. Use the model above to guide your writing.

Evaluative Reports

An evaluative report does more than simply provide information: it analyzes the information and makes recommendations. You may be asked to write an evaluative report to help purchasing decisions or to resolve a procedural problem in the office.

Here are the parts of an evaluative report:

1. The introduction describes what the report is about, who commissioned it, and briefly outlines your conclusions and recommendations.

2. The body of the report begins by filling in the background: present the problem or situation that led to the report being written, along with any other pertinent information or definitions.

3. Next, describe your findings: what methods you used to investigate the issue, and what you found out. For example, if you based your results on a survey, you might explain how many people you polled, what questions you asked, and how you chose your subjects. Try to use descriptive headings in this section to help your readers locate relevant information.

4. Your conclusions section analyzes the results of your investigation.

5. Finally, your recommendations section explains specific actions the company can take to act on the conclusions. Maintain an objective tone when making recommendations. Back up your recommendations with logical, rational arguments, and show how they spring directly from the facts presented in the findings.

File Code: F21

Date: 1995 02 14

Memo To: T.D. Laskin
Director of Education

From: G.C. Petrovsky
Superintendent of Operations
R.D. Adler
Supervisor of Transportation

Re: Cost Benefit Analysis of Board Bus Fleet

Introduction

As requested by the members of the Board of Education, we have examined the issue of whether or not to continue to run the Board of Education's bus fleet. We conclude that the fleet remains the most cost effective and efficient way to meet the Board's transportation needs.

Background

In July, 1994, the Ministry of Education announced it would no longer provide Boards with capital funding for replacement vehicles, effective July 1, 1995. The Ministry also stated that the per diem approval amounts for Board buses would be equated with the amounts provided for contract operators. As a result of these changes, a decision was made to determine if it is economically feasible for the Board to continue to operate its own bus fleet, or whether it should turn its transportation services over to a private operator.

Cost Benefit Analysis

In investigating this issue, we relied heavily on a cost benefit analysis of the board bus fleet (see Appendix A). The figures are taken from actual or projected costs of running the fleet in 1994, 1995, and in the near future. In all three cases, the Board's net operating costs are substantially lower than those of the contract operators. Also, the unrecognized operating costs, for which the Board receives no grants, are substantially lower for the Board buses than they are for the contract operators.

Additional Benefits of a Board Fleet

In addition to the cost advantage of maintaining a Board fleet, some other benefits to this arrangement should be noted:

- A cost-efficient Board-operated fleet is a necessary tool in negotiations with contract bus operators in that the board has the advantage of "having a pulse on the situation."

- The Board is more sensitive to the daily costs and problems concerning the operation of a school bus fleet and is less likely to be taken advantage of by an operator.

- The Board fleet sets high standards for driver safety and vehicle maintenance. Operators must practise the same standards.

- The Board buses provide an opportunity for transportation staff to evaluate the effectiveness of features designed to enhance student safety and/or overall efficiency. The following list gives examples of bus features the Board fleet has tested:

  - Cross-over arms

  - Vista "snub-nosed" buses

  - 78-passenger buses

  - Video camera on buses

  - Back-up alarms

  - Reflective tape

  - In-line diesel engine

  - Disc brakes

  - Larger tail-lights

- The Board fleet ensures that schools receive the best possible field trip rates.

Recommendations

Given these findings, we recommend that the Board continue to operate its fleet of school buses. We further recommend that a similar cost benefit analysis be conducted every three years or after any significant change in the Ministry's transportation grants.

[Note: In the interest of conserving space, Appendix A has not been included in this sample.]

Proposals   A proposal is a report that tries to persuade the reader to do or buy something. You might write a proposal to convince your boss to buy a new piece of machinery to improve productivity, or your company might submit a proposal to a client company to convince them to buy a particular product or service. Proposals can be hundreds of pages long or as short as a paragraph.

> A proposal is a report, so you need to maintain as much objectivity as possible, while at the same time making it clear that the solution you are proposing is the best one possible. Use facts to make your argument for you, and avoid appeals to theories or emotions.

Use the following guidelines to help you organize an informal proposal:

1. The introduction presents highlights from the body of the report. Usually it will include a description of the problem or need and the proposed solution. It should include the total cost of the proposal and the completion date, if applicable.

2. Begin the body of the proposal with background information: describe the problem, and suggest criteria for evaluating possible solutions.

3. Next, describe your proposal. Include relevant information such as how long it will take to implement, how the work will proceed, and how much it will cost. Your proposal will be more convincing if you set out specific criteria for solving the problem, and then show how what you are suggesting fulfills each criterion.

> You may want to present other solutions, and analyze each one according to the criteria you have developed, to show that your proposal is the best.

4. Finally, establish your credibility by describing the qualifications and experience you or your company has in the field.

5. You may choose to end with a summary of the benefits to be derived from your proposal. You can be less objective in this final section, but don't go overboard in selling your idea. Maintain a formal tone.

Request for Funding

To: Friends of the Environment Foundation
From: The Ontario Public Interest Research Group, Guelph

Introduction

We are requesting funding in order to refurbish and improve a very popular interactive display, designed to educate the public about "green" environmental practices in the home. The estimated total cost of the project is $7596.72. After receiving a donation of some display panels, we still need $4596.72. Construction of the display would begin in April (or earlier if a part-time coordinator is hired) and be completed by the end of May.

Background

In 1989, OPIRG-Guelph developed an extremely popular educational display called the Urban House of Horrors. The display is a mock-up of a house with real fixtures (bath, toilet, stove, etc.). Individuals walk into the display as they would rooms of their own home and are presented with information, in a variety of forms, that provides practical and simple alternatives to common household activities that are detrimental to the environment. There are flaps to lift, quizzes and puzzles to solve, and buzzer boards to press. Literature is provided for individuals to take home with them.

During the summer of 1990, we conducted an ambitious door-to-door environmental survey in Guelph. Over 8000 households were visited and over 1500 environmental surveys were collected. This project provided us with important background research on what people need to make their lives more environmentally friendly. We learned that people were very eager to make a difference but still lacked friendly accessible ways of obtaining information to make the necessary educated choices in their lifestyle.

Proposal

We are seeking funds to improve on our prototype for the Urban House of Horrors. The concept is fully developed, but we want to make it more professional looking and lightweight, so that it can be easily moved and set up. The condition of the current display has deteriorated, and we would like to make a new model that would stand up to a lot of use.

Rationale

The barrage of environmental disasters and problems can be overwhelming for most people. It is often difficult to see how individuals can have an impact on problems as large as global warming. The importance of the Urban House of Horrors display is that it shows how individuals can make significant contributions to their local and global environment.

The Urban House of Horrors is an interactive display that has proven popular with both adults and children of all ages. The display is fun, and yet manages to convey an enormous amount of information. The positive feedback that we have received about the display is evidence of the fact that it is an extremely accessible way of presenting information. We have received many requests to exhibit our display both within and outside Guelph, but because of its unwieldy size, we have not often been able to comply.

Uses of the Display

The display will first be shown at the Guelph Spring Festival Block Party on May 23, with an expected attendance of between 3000 and 4000 people from Guelph. The display will then go into a mall (Stone Road Mall, Eaton Centre, or Willow West Mall) as part of National Environment Week (June 1 to 7) activities in Guelph. The display will be used at numerous community events, particularly during the summer.

During the fall and winter, we would like to book the display into schools. We have talked to several area teachers involved in environmental education, and they are extremely excited about setting up the display in their schools. We would concentrate on school bookings in Guelph initially, and slowly extend our range into adjacent municipalities.

Costs

Project coordinator	2560.00 (1)
Benefits	286.72 (2)
Display Panels	3000.00
Materials and Supplies	1000.00 (3)
Printing and Promotion	750.00 (4)
Total Expenses	7596.72
In-kind contribution	3000.00 (5)
Request from Friends of the Environment Foundation	4596.72

Budget Notes

(1) The project coordinator's position will be full time for a period of 8 weeks at $8.00/hour (or alternatively a half-time position for 16 weeks). The coordinator will be responsible for developing the display, coordinating volunteers, and organizing the staffing and set-up of the display at the Block Party.

(2) Benefits include Unemployment Insurance, Canada Pension Plan, Employer's Health Tax and vacation pay (4%).

(3) Materials and supplies (e.g., cardboard, Bristol board, laminating, etc.) to rebuild components of the display.

(4) Printing of educational materials and promotion of the display.

(5) We have received a contribution of modular display panels and travelling cases.

Staffing

We are a volunteer organization. We have two permanent staff and a variable number of grant staff. We have a volunteer board of students and community members and numerous volunteers working on a wide variety of issues. This kind of project will draw on the ideas and advice of many of these people and the project coordinator will be responsible for coordinating volunteer contributions to the project. At least one of the permanent staff will be involved in supervising the project. Depending on the various granting agencies, we may also have grant staff to assist on various aspects of the display. Certainly, we will have numerous people to draw on to staff the display at the Block Party and during Environment Week.

Schedule

We would like to begin the project in April (or February if we have someone part time for 16 weeks) and finish at the end of May for the Guelph Spring Festival Block Party.

Credentials

We have enclosed a copy of our last progress report which describes our organization and the type of projects that we work on.

Used with permission of the Ontario Public Interest Research Group, Guelph.

FORMAL REPORTS

Anything that is the subject of an informal report can be made the subject of a formal report, but most formal reports are proposals (to perform a service for a client company, to improve operations within the company) or evaluations (of a process or product, for example).

- Formal reports are usually written for an outside audience or for top executives within the company, while informal reports are most often for internal circulation.

- Formal reports tend to be longer, more detailed, and more complex than informal reports.

- They follow a set pattern. In addition to the actual report, which follows the same pattern as an informal report, a formal report includes most or all of the following elements:
  FRONT MATTER
  Letter of Transmittal
  Title Page
  Summary, Executive Summary, or Abstract
  Table of Contents
  List of Figures (and/or Illustrations)

  BACK MATTER
  Works Cited
  Bibliography
  Appendices

Letter of Transmittal

The letter of transmittal is usually clipped to the outside front cover of the report. Its purpose is to let the principal readers of the report know what they have in their hands. It is often the first part of the report to be read. Include the following information in your letter of transmittal:

1. Describe what the report is about, who commissioned it, and when.

2. Summarize the main parts of the report, or draw attention to particularly important findings.

3. Acknowledge any help you had in preparing the report.

4. Offer assistance in answering any questions about the report.

CROSS-REFERENCE

▶ Proper letter formats are described earlier in this chapter, beginning on page 140.

Friends of the Environment Foundation
763 Smith Road
Guelph, Ontario
N1H 4N4

January 7, 1996

Dear Sir or Madam:

Enclosed is a request for funding by the Ontario Public Interest Research Group, Guelph to improve an educational environmental display called the "Urban House of Horrors." This interactive display is designed to educate the public regarding ways to make their own household more environmentally friendly. A prototype of the display has already proved to be an extremely popular and effective way of transmitting environmental information to the community.

We need funds to improve the prototype, making it more lightweight and durable, so it can be moved from site to site easily. These improvements would allow us to use the display at festivals and community events in the summer and in schools during the winter.

The project would begin in April and finish by the end of May. The total cost of the project is estimated at $7596.72. We have already received a donation in kind of $3000.00. Therefore, we are requesting a grant of $4596.72 to cover the cost of hiring a project coordinator and purchasing necessary materials and supplies.

I would like to thank you for your consideration and look forward to hearing from you. If you have any questions about our project please do not hesitate to call me.

Yours sincerely,

Kara Farley

Kara Farley
Coordinator

Title Page The title page of your report should include:

1. the title of the report;

2. the name and title of the person or company it was prepared for;

3. the name and title of the person who prepared it and the company she or he works for;

4. the date of transmittal.

CROSS-REFERENCE

▶ For a sample title page from a report, see page 90.

Summary Your purpose in writing the summary is to make the information in the report accessible to executives who have no time to read it from cover to cover. Include information from each main section of the report, and keep the length down to under a page. The summary is sometimes called an "Executive Summary." In technical or scientific reports, it is called an "Abstract."

The summary is perhaps the most important part of your whole report. In fact, it may be the only part of your report that will be read closely by some readers. Write it after you have written the final draft of your report.

Table of Contents and List of Figures See page 90 for instructions on how to prepare a table of contents and list of figures or tables.

Works Cited and Bibliography Use in-text citations to document your sources in a report. The works cited list should include all references cited in the body of the report. The bibliography lists all references you consulted in writing the report, including those not actually cited in the body of the report. Both lists use the same format.

CROSS-REFERENCE

▶ For an explanation of how to use in-text citations and how to prepare a list of works cited, see page 125.

Appendices If you are using charts, graphs, or any documents to support your research, you can either work them into the body of the report or place them in appendices at the end of the report, labelled Appendix A, Appendix B, etc. If the material is very long or very technical, it is usually better to put it in an appendix.

CROSS-REFERENCE

▶ For more information on how to use graphs and charts, see page 85.

Make reference to the material at an appropriate place in the body of the report so your readers know it is there, and can turn to it if they wish. Begin each appendix on a separate page.

SCIENTIFIC REPORTS

Scientific reports are based on experimentation and data collection. This sample table of contents illustrates the structure and main elements of a formal scientific report.

If you are writing a formal laboratory report, check with your teacher for the format she or he prefers.

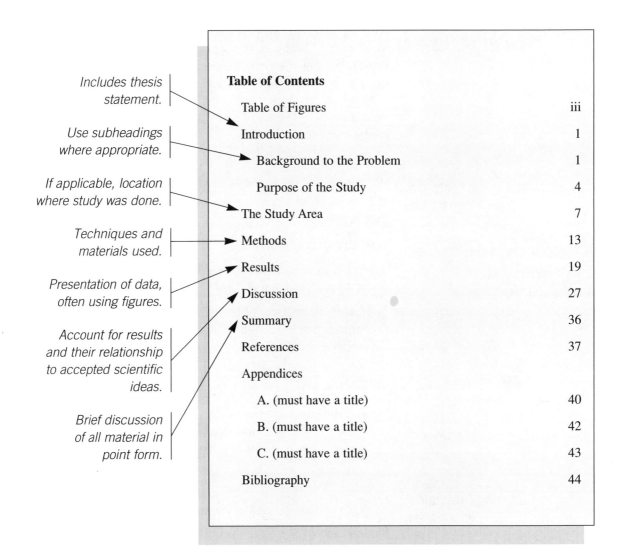

Includes thesis statement.

Use subheadings where appropriate.

If applicable, location where study was done.

Techniques and materials used.

Presentation of data, often using figures.

Account for results and their relationship to accepted scientific ideas.

Brief discussion of all material in point form.

Table of Contents

CHECKLIST FOR WRITING REPORTS

Have I:

☑ Included information that is appropriate to my audience and purpose?

☑ Placed the most important information at the beginning?

☑ Written formally and objectively?

☑ Included the front and back matter that is appropriate to the degree of formality of my report?

☑ Used headings to break up the text and to guide my reader?

☑ Attached any important documentation?

TECHNO TRANSFER

With the fast rate of technological changes in business, knowing how to understand and convey specialized or technical information is more important than ever before. Without good communication skills, experts and non-experts in a particular field can find it very difficult to communicate. *Techno transfer* is a recently developed term that describes the process of conveying technical information to a non-expert audience.

Understanding Technical Information

Here are some tips to help you approach technical information. Many of them apply to any situation in which you are listening or reading to gain information.

CROSS-REFERENCE

▶ For more details on reading techniques, see page 209.

• Read with a purpose.

• Begin by looking at any headings and subheadings, and thinking or listing what you already know about or associate with them.

• Look for a glossary of terms. If there is one, skim through it quickly before you read, then refer to it whenever you come to an unfamiliar term.

• Decide whether what you are reading is describing a process, procedure, or thing (e.g., a piece of machinery).

• List questions or terms you do not understand. If you still do not know the answers after reading through the entire document, do some research, or ask someone knowledgeable to explain it to you.

Conveying Technical Information

How would you describe how to tie a shoelace to someone who grew up with Velcro®? Suddenly, a simple process with which you are very familiar becomes a complex, multi-step procedure. Here are some steps to help you address an audience that is unfamiliar with your subject matter.

- Avoid jargon. When you do use technical language to identify specific terms or parts, be sure to define your terms in the text. If the document contains a lot of technical terms, consider adding a glossary at the end of the document.

- Use visual aids, such as labelled illustrations, charts, flowcharts, and graphs to make information easier to understand.

- Use clear and informative headings and subheadings in written material. Your readers will use the headings to help them get an overview of the subject matter.

- Use analogies to make unfamiliar concepts or processes more accessible.

- Use the active voice.

Weak: Connecting the two wires is done with pliers.
Better: Connect the two wires using pliers.

Weak: A decision should be made regarding which contractor to hire.
Better: We should decide which contractor to hire.

- Emphasize the important subjects and verbs. Construct sentences so that the main verb is the most important verb, and the subject of the sentence is the most important noun.

Weak: *Containment* of the effluent is important.
Better: We must *contain* the effluent.

Weak: The *role* of the co-processor is to help the main processor perform certain functions, such as mathematical calculations.
Better: The *co-processor* helps the main processor to perform certain functions, such as mathematical calculations.

- Link parallel ideas, steps, or objects using parallel constructions.

The following sections contain guidelines for communicating unfamiliar terms or procedures to an audience.

CROSS-REFERENCE

▶ Active and passive voice are explained on page 45.

CROSS-REFERENCE

▶ See *Parallelism*, page 40.

Defining a Term

When you are explaining technical information to a lay audience, it is particularly important that you define your terms clearly. Here are some steps to follow in formulating useful definitions.

1. Start by explaining what general class of things or ideas the term belongs to.

   A ptarmigan is a member of the grouse family.

   A camshaft is a long shaft.

A radius is a line segment.

An optical scanner is a piece of computer hardware.

2. Then describe the features of the term that differentiate it from others in the same general class.

A ptarmigan is the only member of the grouse family that has snow white winter plumage.

The camshaft is a long shaft with knobs, or cams, protruding from it at intervals.

A radius is a line segment that joins the centre of a circle to a point on the circumference.

An optical scanner is a piece of hardware that allows a computer to read handwritten or typed material.

3. If necessary, add further information about the term that is relevant to your audience and purpose. Think of who, when, where, what, and how questions that your audience might need or want answered. For example:

What does it look like? (Describe and/or include a graphic representation of the item)
What parts does it have?
What is it similar to?
What is it different from?
What is its significance?
What features does it have?
What is an example?
Where does it come from?
When is it used?
Who made/discovered it?
How is it used?
How does it work?

Diagrams, photographs, or other graphic representations can be very helpful when you are defining parts of machinery or equipment.

CHECKLIST FOR WRITING DEFINITIONS

Have I:

☑ Described the item or idea accurately and completely?

☑ Written a definition that distinguishes my subject matter from other similar items or ideas?

☑ Avoided using terms that my audience will be unfamiliar with in my definition?

☑ Used graphics or visuals if necessary and appropriate?

☑ Answered my readers' questions about the item or idea?

Explaining a Process or Procedure

Writing good instructions is a fine art, as anyone who has tried to program their VCR knows. You could be asked to write instructions explaining how to use a piece of machinery, or how to perform a particular function. Here are some tips to help you.

1. Begin by listing all the tools and materials needed to complete the task.

2. Define the terminology (names of parts, etc.) that you will be referring to in your instructions. Often the best way to do this is with a labelled illustration like the one below.

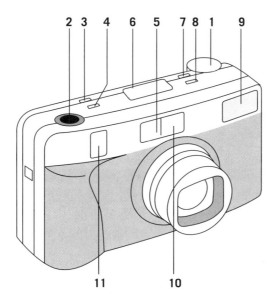

1 Zooming lever.
2 Shutter release button.
3 Drive button.
4 Infinity-landscape button.
5 Autofocus window.
6 LCD panel.
7 Mode button.
8 Red-eye reduction flash button.
9 Built-in flash.
10 Viewfinder window.
11 Light sensor window.

3. Number each step.

4. Do not include too much information in each step.

Confusing: Form a loop with the string in your left hand, making sure that you have 2–3 cm of string left dangling. Pinch the base of the loop between your left thumb and index finger, and circle the right hand string counterclockwise around the base of the loop. This new loop is called the encircling loop.

Better: *1.* Form a loop with the string in your left hand, making sure that you have 2–3 cm of string left dangling. This loop is called the left loop.
2. Pinch the base of the left loop between your left thumb and index finger.
3. Circle the right hand string counterclockwise around the base of the loop. This new loop is called the encircling loop.

CROSS-REFERENCE

▶ The passive voice is explained on page 44.

5. Whenever possible, start each sentence with a verb. Avoid the passive voice and the phrase "you should."

Weak: A right loop is then formed by passing a piece of the right-hand lace under the encircling loop to the right of the left loop.

Weak: You should form a loop near the end of the right hand lace, and pass it underneath the encircling loop to the right of the left loop. This new loop is called the right loop.

Better: Form a loop near the end of the right hand lace and pass it underneath the encircling loop to the right of the left loop. This new loop is called the right loop.

> Try performing the actions as you write to remind yourself of the steps involved.

6. Keep your terminology as simple and consistent as possible. While repeating words and phrases over and over is not usually desirable, it is better to repeat the same word than to confuse your reader with too many synonyms.

> One way to avoid repeating long tedious phrases is to give names to particular parts of the process. In the previous examples, note how the author names the different loops (left loop, encircling loop, right loop) to make it easier to distinguish them in later instructions.

Weak: Hold the top of the right hand bow between the right thumb and index finger, and the left loop between the left thumb and index finger. Pull both sides outwards gently, until the encircling loop tightens. Do not allow the ends of the laces to pass through the middle loop.

Better: Hold the top of the right *loop* between the right thumb and forefinger and the top of the left loop between the left thumb and index finger. Pull both *loops* outwards gently, until the encircling loop tightens. Do not allow the ends of the *laces* to pass through the encircling loop.

CROSS-REFERENCE

▶ If you are explaining a process in front of an audience, refer to the section on *Demonstrations*, on page 186.

7. Often, a graphic is the best way to convey instructions. Imagine how much simpler it would be to explain how to tie a shoelace if you could use diagrams as well as words.

APPLY IT!

Write a set of instructions explaining how to do one of the following. Include visuals, if they are appropriate, to supplement your written description.

- Parallel park a car.

- Change a car or bicycle tire.

- Say the word "bit." (Assume your reader knows how to make sounds but has never pronounced an English word before. Luckily, he or she can read English instructions with ease.)

- French braid your own hair.

- Draw the following pattern (no visuals allowed for this one):

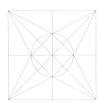

CHECKLIST FOR WRITING CLEAR INSTRUCTIONS

Have I:

- ☑ Listed all the tools and materials necessary to perform the task?

- ☑ Defined any technical or unfamiliar words for my readers?

- ☑ Broken the process down into manageable steps?

- ☑ Phrased each command clearly, using the active voice, and beginning with a verb whenever possible?

- ☑ Used graphics when appropriate to supplement my written instructions?

- ☑ Tried following my own instructions to make sure nothing is missing?

LISTENING AND SPEAKING

Although we practise the skills of listening and speaking every day of our lives, most of us have a lot to learn about communicating orally. This chapter will prepare you for everything from listening to a close friend to speaking in public.

CONTENTS

EFFECTIVE LISTENING

Effective listening means being an *active* listener, not just a passive observer. Listening well involves more than your ears; your eyes, your body posture, your hands, and your mind all have to be involved in the process. Sound odd? Read on...

Listening Well: Steps for Success

The key to listening well is *concentration*. Here are some tips to help you maintain your level of concentration.

STEP 1: *Listen with your whole body.*
Start by tuning out distractions. Keep your eyes focused on the speaker. Make sure that your body posture shows that you are relaxed but alert. Don't slouch!

The person who is talking is usually influenced by how you listen. (Have you ever tried to give a speech in front of a hostile crowd?) If you show your interest, you help the speaker to say clearly what she or he has in mind. Looking directly at the speaker will help you pick up the more subtle messages conveyed by body language.

CROSS-REFERENCE

▶ See *Making Notes in Lectures or Discussions* on page 182.

Another way to get your body involved in the listening process is to take notes. Of course, notes are also useful afterwards to remind you of what was said. But try to write down only the main points. Don't get so caught up in your writing that you miss the main attraction.

STEP 2: *Listen for a reason.*
You can listen for all sorts of reasons: to get information, to be entertained, to broaden your understanding, or to get closer to a friend. Here are a few reasons why you might listen to another person, and some actions you can take to keep yourself focused on your goal.

REASON FOR LISTENING	EXAMPLE	PLAN FOR ACTIVE LISTENING
To gather information.	science lecture	• Write down main ideas. • Make note of questions that occur to you. • Review or transcribe notes soon after the event to clear up misunderstandings early.
To get help in forming an opinion.	a political debate	• Make note of main ideas. • Consider the overall meaning of what is said. • Critically analyze the validity of each point. • Be prepared to ask questions.

REASON FOR LISTENING	EXAMPLE	PLAN FOR ACTIVE LISTENING
To develop closeness.	a friend	• Try to understand the other person's needs, personality, and point of view. Relate them to your own past experience. • Ask questions that show interest in and understanding of the other person.

Don't let the speaker lead you around like a dog on a leash. If you are listening with a purpose, you will know what to listen for, and may be able to anticipate where the speaker is taking you.

STEP 3: *Pick up the speaker's signals.*

When we listen, we tend to pay attention for about thirty seconds at a time, then drift away for a while before returning our concentration to the speaker. This makes it almost impossible to pick up every word that is said. The trick is to listen and watch for clues that will give you a sense of the big picture and help redirect your attention when it wanders. Here are some clues to be aware of:

• Try to pick out the main ideas in the lecture or talk. A speech has structure, just as a written essay does. Your job is to discover that structure.

• Words like "firstly," "next," or "finally," often indicate a series of important points.

• Listen for sentences like "There are three ways of going about this," "I will present four reasons why...". They let you know what is coming.

• Pay attention to the speaker's body language. Body language is the way we communicate through gestures, facial expressions, and movements. For example, if your teacher suddenly stops pacing, wags a finger, makes eye contact, or turns around from the blackboard, he or she is probably doing so to emphasize an important point.

Even if you are listening to a speech in a huge auditorium, try to listen as if you and the speaker are alone in the room, having a private conversation. Think about how you would respond to each point being made.

Barriers to Listening

Being an effective listener also means not letting barriers interfere with your listening.

- Try to block out all distractions.

- Listen for the main ideas and note the details later.

- Avoid getting emotionally upset and presenting arguments before the speaker is finished.

- Evaluate *what* is said, not *how* it is said. Avoid criticizing the speaker's personality or manner of presentation.

Making Notes in Lectures or Discussions

Some people have trouble taking notes in lectures or discussions because they try to write down *everything* a speaker says. Three key points are worth remembering.

1. Aim to write down only the *main ideas* of a lecture or discussion.

2. Try to spend more time listening than writing. Think about what you hear *before* you write it down.

3. Ask yourself *questions* about the main ideas presented. Write them down so you can ask the speaker to answer them.

A P P L Y I T !

▶ *Look over your notes from a past lecture or discussion and evaluate your note-taking ability using the guidelines given here. How could you improve your skill in taking notes?*

EFFECTIVE SPEAKING

Here are three steps that will help you to be a success in public speaking:

STEP 1: *Be prepared.*
This step is designed to help you use your time efficiently as you work through the next two steps.

(a) Begin by learning all you can about the *context* in which you will speak. Ask yourself:
  - Is it a debate? A prepared speech by me alone? A panel discussion? A meeting?

- Will I be expected to ask questions? Answer questions?
- Will the room in which I speak be too large for posters or illustrations to be used? Will there be a microphone—and if so, can I practise with it in advance?
- Will there be a fixed time limit for my comments or presentation?

(b) Next, learn all you can about your *topic*.
- If you are to give a speech, anticipate possible questions and plan how you will answer.
- If you are to be the chairperson of a discussion, talk with each of the participants and learn what kinds of information each will have to offer and what role each is likely to play.
- If you are participating in a debate, coordinate your presentation with your partner's and anticipate the arguments of the opposing side.

STEP 2: *Know your purpose and your audience.*
Once you know about the context in which you will be speaking and about the topic of the discussion, decide on your *purpose* (so you will know what to say) and your *audience* (so you will know how to say it). Here are some examples:

PURPOSE	WHAT TO SAY
To present a science project.	• Describe project plan and format. • Provide facts. • Give findings. • Explain conclusions.
To open a meeting.	• Welcome the group. • List topics to be discussed. • Follow any club procedures.
To deliver a speech to persuade school officials.	• State a position with facts. • Give arguments to support your position. • Address any contrary opinions openly. • Restate your position firmly.

AUDIENCE	HOW TO SAY IT
Your own science class.	• Draw upon information known to the class as a whole. • Highlight anything not familiar to the class. • Be well organized, concise, and relaxed.
Members of your photography club.	• Be relaxed and casual; you are among friends. • Know what you are going to say, but remember it is an informal meeting; the group has gathered by choice and for recreation. • Feel free to use slang, but don't joke around so much that nothing is accomplished.
School officials and members of the community.	• Be formal, concise, and well prepared. • Be highly respectful of your audience but not too modest or apologetic. • Stick rigorously to the topic.

STEP 3: *Practise your delivery.*

The best way to practise is with an audience. If you cannot enlist friends or family members to comment on your delivery, be your own audience and practise in front of a mirror. If you have access to video equipment, tape yourself and evaluate your speech on tape. Here is what to aim for in your presentation:

• Be confident, relaxed, and enthusiastic about your topic, even if all you feel like doing is running from the building. Your audience is looking to you for cues. If you act bored by your subject, expect your listeners to be bored too.

> Make a conscious effort to keep your shoulders down rather than hunched up and tense. This will help you to both look and feel relaxed. It works! Try it!

• Be conscious of mannerisms that could distract your audience, such as clearing your throat or chopping the air with your hand. Stand straight, but not rigid, and find something to keep your hands occupied (holding your notes, or placing your hands on the lectern, for example). Gesturing and moving about are fine, but do them smoothly and in appropriate places. Sudden lunges or nervous tics will steal the show.

• Use gestures, eye contact, and the tone of your voice to alert your listeners to important statements or to indicate when you are making a new point.

- When you are delivering your speech, focus your eyes briefly on individuals in the audience. This will help you to overcome your nervousness, and to act more naturally. It will also help to engage your listeners. Be sure to cover the whole room, and move from one person to another fairly often so you don't make anyone nervous by staring at them for too long.

- Speak loudly and distinctly enough to be heard by everyone in the room. Avoid saying "um" or "er" too often.

> Try listening to yourself on tape. Make note of the tone of your voice, how fast you are speaking, and how often you say "um." Also listen for places where you could make your language more vivid.

- Slow down! Most people tend to talk too fast, and rush through their words. Make a conscious effort to speak more slowly.

- Pause occasionally to give your listeners time to digest an important point or to mark a break between topics.

Using Visual and Audio Aids in a Speech

You can also use visual or audio aids to increase the impact of a speech.

- Don't use props for their own sake. Be sure that they are helping your audience to grasp your message, rather than diverting their attention.

- Practise how to use illustrations, including how to point to them or to particular aspects of them, until you feel completely comfortable.

- Make sure everyone in your audience can see and understand the illustrations. Leave them up long enough for everyone to absorb the information. Use a pointer, and never stand between your audience and the visuals.

- Keep your eyes focused on your audience, not on the illustrations or the equipment.

> You can create professional-looking charts and graphs for overheads using a personal computer. Create the artwork on the computer and print it out. Then photocopy the image onto a sheet of acetate.

- Be sure all the technical equipment you need (CD players, overhead projectors, etc.) is working well, and that you know how to use it. Adjust the volume control before you begin the presentation.

Demonstrations

Demonstrations are very similar to illustrated talks. They are common in science, technical, and art classes. Here are some guidelines for giving a demonstration.

- Begin by explaining the overall purpose of the demonstration.

- Show the audience each of the articles you will use in the demonstration.

- At each step of the demonstration, make certain that everyone in the audience has a chance to see exactly what you are doing. When possible, carry a portion of the demonstration into the centre of the audience. This method involves the audience in the presentation.

- Practise in advance so you can talk naturally while you are demonstrating.

CROSS-REFERENCE

▶ For tips on how to explain a process, see page 175.

LISTENING AND SPEAKING IN GROUPS

You probably already have lots of experience working in groups. Sometimes, working with others can be rewarding. Other times, the group just doesn't seem to get anything done. Good groups are built on good communication, mutual trust, and a shared goal. Here are some tips that can make a difference.

CROSS-REFERENCE

▶ See page 180 for more on active listening.

- Listen actively. Use the tips given earlier in this chapter.

- Let everyone have their say. Take it upon yourself to invite a group member who has not said much to participate. You can say "Joachim, what do you think about this issue?" or "Asra, we haven't heard from you yet."

- Give praise where praise is due. Acknowledge the contributions of individual members ("Thanks for getting all that information from the library, Jolene."); encourage members who come up with ideas ("That's an interesting approach, Marco. Tell us more."); and never, never make fun of what another member says. Nothing is more likely to discourage involvement than put-downs and sarcasm.

- Don't interrupt. If you find it difficult to get a word in, try the good old-fashioned method of putting up your hand so people know you want to speak next. More subtle cues, such as sitting forward in your seat or catching the eye of the chairperson, are preferable but may take some practice.

> The exception to the "don't interrupt" rule is when a group member is taking up too much time, or going off topic. Try saying something like, "Excuse me, but I think we need to concentrate on the main point of the discussion," or "Excuse me, Barb, but I think Ali had something to say about that. Ali?"

Dealing with Disagreements

Most groups go through a growth period when members feel dissatisfied with the way things are going. In most cases, this stage passes, and the group starts to work together well. However, if you find you are having trouble with a particular group member, remember the following:

- Don't take discussions personally. Disagreeing with someone's idea is not the same as disliking them. When someone disagrees with something you have said, listen to what they have to say, and keep an open mind. Don't decide that they just don't like you.

- Don't make discussions personal. If you are disagreeing with an idea, make friendly eye contact with the person who presented the idea, keep your voice calm, and don't lean away or cross your arms (these may make the person think you are not interested in discussing the point). Try to phrase your disagreement clearly but impersonally. For example, never say "I disagree with you." Instead, say "I disagree with the idea that..." Then, be prepared to listen and to change your mind. Maybe they are right after all.

- Use sentences that start with "I feel." If you talk about how other people's words or actions make you *feel*, rather than talking about their words or actions themselves, you will sound much less aggressive, and you will make it easier for the other person to respond positively. For example, if someone in the group does not seem to be pulling his or her weight, you could say "You're just loafing around and breaking up the group." But if you say "I feel uncomfortable when people in the group don't participate," you accept partial responsibility for the situation, and leave room for the other person to respond positively.

- Find common ground. Without a common goal, you would not be together as a group. Remind yourselves of what that goal is. Focusing on what you have to do together to accomplish it may help you to set aside your differences, at least temporarily.

- Split into subgroups. Research has shown that groups tend to work best when they are small (three or four members). If you find that some members of the group are not working as hard on a project as others, consider breaking up into smaller groups with specific tasks assigned to each unit, and meeting with the larger group less often.

A P P L Y I T !

▶ *You are a member of a group of six students who are supposed to be working together on a science project. The group is not working well. Only a few members seem to be doing any work. The rest attend the meetings but do not contribute much. No one is very happy with the situation but, so far, it has not been discussed. Explain in detail how you would deal with this situation.*

Brainstorming

Brainstorming is a way of encouraging creative ideas in order to solve a specific problem. The aims of brainstorming are to produce as many ideas as possible and to produce more creative solutions than might otherwise be possible. Brainstorming is a good way to get the ball rolling if you are having trouble thinking of a topic for a project, for example, or want to get a new angle on a problem. Here is how to brainstorm:

1. Have the chairperson introduce the topic and state the problem.

2. Have someone stand at the front of the group and write down all the ideas that are generated on a blackboard or sheet of paper. If possible, make sure all members can see the ideas that are written down.

3. Do not judge or reject any of the ideas presented. Even if an idea sounds impractical or silly, it may stimulate the creativity of someone else. It is up to the chairperson to catch anyone who starts to express an opinion about the feasibility of an idea.

4. Aim for quantity, not quality. Encourage each member to present as many ideas as possible and to build on other members' ideas.

5. Have your own group or another group narrow down the ideas generated and analyze each remaining proposal in detail.

Before you reject the more bizarre ideas, try to translate them into more workable solutions. For example, if you are brainstorming ways to raise money for an exchange trip, the idea "we could get Blue Rodeo to do a benefit concert in the school auditorium" might lead you to the more practical suggestion of putting on your own benefit concert, including impersonations of famous people, or of getting a local band to do a benefit.

Committees A committee is made up of a small group of people who have been asked to work on behalf of a larger group. You might want to form a committee:

- to solve a problem;
- to gather information;
- to monitor an ongoing situation;
- to initiate and carry out a specific task (such as selling tickets).

CROSS-REFERENCE

▶ See also *Role of the Chairperson*, page 193.

Each time a committee meets, there is a group discussion. It helps if the committee has a chairperson and if each member has a specific area to report on.

CHECKLIST FOR COMMITTEE MEETINGS

Did we:

☑ Begin by defining the purpose of the discussion?

☑ Stick to the topic?

☑ Give each member a chance to speak?

☑ Come up with a workable plan or solution?

Panels A panel is made up of three to seven people who are knowledgeable about a specific topic. Most panel discussions have a chairperson or moderator. In a panel discussion, the panelists sit before an audience and talk among themselves in voices loud enough to be heard by the audience. The audience has the opportunity to hear differing points of view on a topic. Many panel discussions allow for a question period at the end. During the question period, members of the audience ask questions directed either at an individual panel member or at the panel as a whole.

CHECKLIST FOR PANEL DISCUSSIONS

Did the panel members:

☑ Come to the discussion well-informed about the topic?

☑ Speak loudly enough for the audience to hear?

☑ Respect each other's opinions and avoid interrupting?

Did the audience:

☑ Listen attentively to each speaker and try to separate fact from opinion?

☑ Come prepared to ask questions of the panel members?

Symposiums   A symposium is a gathering of well-informed individuals, each of whom is prepared to give a formal presentation on a specific aspect of a chosen subject. The presentations are usually given before an audience, but unlike a panel discussion, participants in a symposium don't necessarily discuss the issue in front of the audience.

A symposium is usually chaired by one person, who introduces the participants and explains their areas of expertise. Usually, there is a question period after each presentation.

CHECKLIST FOR SYMPOSIUMS

Did I:

☑ Come to the symposium ready to speak in depth on the topic assigned?

☑ Come with some knowledge of the other topics to be covered, to be able to ask and respond to questions?

☑ Listen attentively to each speaker, and try to ask meaningful questions of him or her?

☑ Try to compare and evaluate the different points of view of the participants?

Forums   A forum is a group discussion in which everyone has an opportunity to express views or ask questions. Usually one topic is designated for review. Often a panel will provide information or opinions in response to formal questions from the audience. The job of the chairperson or moderator of a forum is to call upon members of the audience and direct questions to the appropriate panel members.

CHECKLIST FOR FORUM PARTICIPANTS

Did I:

☑ Stick to the topic?

☑ Listen carefully to each person who spoke?

☑ Wait for the chairperson to recognize me before I spoke?

Formal Meetings

A meeting is usually a regular gathering of people who belong to a club or organization. A meeting can be either formal or informal.

A formal meeting is conducted by a chairperson according to the rules of parliamentary procedure. It follows a specific plan, or agenda, prepared and distributed in advance by the chairperson. Most formal meetings follow this pattern:

CROSS-REFERENCE

▶ See also *Committees*, page 189.

1. Call to order by the chairperson.

2. Reading or distribution of the minutes of the previous meeting. (The *minutes* are the official record of what happened at the meeting.)

3. Reports of various committees.

4. Unfinished business from previous meetings.

5. New business.

6. Announcements.

7. Adjournment by the chairperson.

All remarks in a formal meeting are directed at the chairperson.

Decisions in a formal meeting are made by motions followed by voting. A motion is a formal suggestion put before the group for consideration, such as "I move that we adopt a pet rat as our school mascot."

Here is the process by which a motion leads to a decision by the group.

1. The person making the motion begins his or her statement by saying, "I move that...."

2. A motion requires a seconder, a person who agrees that this motion is a good idea. The seconder says, "I second the motion."

3. A discussion of the motion follows. Anyone wishing to speak raises her or his hand to address the chairperson.

4. When discussion seems near an end, the chairperson will ask, "Is there any further discussion?" If not, voting follows. Generally, motions are voted on by a show of hands. The chairperson only votes if there is a tie.

For more information on parliamentary procedure, look over a copy of *Robert's Rules of Order.* Most libraries have this book.

> To find out what a formal meeting is like, attend a local city council meeting.

CHECKLIST FOR FORMAL MEETINGS

Did we:

☑ Make sure everyone understood how the meeting would proceed before we began?

☑ Come to the meeting prepared to contribute and to listen to other participants?

☑ Stick to the topic and respect the direction of the chairperson?

Informal Debates

A debate is a way of presenting the arguments for and against a subject. When you take part in a debate, your aim is to *defend a position*, regardless of what you may personally feel about the issue.

The rules for formal debates can be found in several books in the library. This section will explain how to stage an informal debate, designed to involve everyone present.

Here is a five-stage plan for an informal classroom debate:

STAGE 1: *Decide on a Resolution*
Present the topic (often called a resolution) as a simple, positive statement, preceded by the words "Be it resolved that..." Make the resolution as specific as possible. Here is an example:

> "Be it resolved that people who choose to smoke should be responsible for their own health care costs."

STAGE 2: *Present the Opposing Views*
Choose four members of the class to present the arguments in the debate. These people will have to do research and prepare their statements before the class meets to debate. Two of them will take the affirmative side. The other two will take the negative side. That is, they will disagree with the statement made in the resolution. The two sides alternate, each member presenting a five-minute speech, while the audience listens and evaluates their arguments.

STAGE 3: *Refute the Arguments*
Each member of the debating team has a few minutes in which to refute, or prove incorrect, the arguments put forward by their opponents.

STAGE 4: *Question Period*

For ten minutes, members of the audience are given a chance to ask questions of the debaters. The chairperson should call on those who want to ask questions.

STAGE 5: *Vote*

At the end of the question period, the chairperson asks the audience to vote by a show of hands to decide which side has won the debate.

C H E C K L I S T   F O R   I N F O R M A L   D E B A T E S

As a debater, did I:

- ☑ Come fully prepared?
- ☑ Rely on facts and sound reasoning to support my point of view?
- ☑ Anticipate the arguments of the opposing side?
- ☑ Anticipate the questions of the audience?
- ☑ Stick to the topic and respect the time limitations?

As a member of the audience, did I:

- ☑ Listen with an open mind?
- ☑ Listen objectively?
- ☑ Make a decision based on the arguments, rather than on personalities?
- ☑ Come with prepared questions?
- ☑ Stick to the topic and respect the time limitations?

Role of the Chairperson

C R O S S - R E F E R E N C E

▶ See also *Formal Meetings*, page 191.

Group discussions are usually more productive if there is a chairperson. This person:

- prepares and distributes an agenda or outline in advance;
- makes an opening statement, setting forth the purpose of the discussion;
- gives each person a chance to participate;
- ensures that participants stick to the subject;
- encourages participants to show courtesy and respect for others;
- provides a summary at the end of the discussion or at any time during the discussion when it might be helpful.

INTERVIEWS

An interview can be a good way to get information. You may want to interview people when you are preparing reports or projects for school, and you will probably be interviewed when you apply for a job. Here are some guidelines for each case.

Research Interviews

1. Establish a plan.
   - Decide who is the best person to ask about the subject you are interested in.
   - Write or call that person to arrange for the interview. Tell the person why you would like the interview, and make an appointment to meet at a convenient time.
   - Prepare a list of questions and arrange them in logical order. Phrase the questions so that the person will give a full answer, not simply yes or no. Be clear and specific about what you want to know.
   - Bring a clipboard or a hardback notebook so that you can take notes without a table. Bring enough paper and pencils so that you won't run out.
   - If possible, bring a tape recorder along. Ask your interview subject if he or she minds you using it. Make sure the batteries are strong and that you know how to use the machine before you arrive at the interview. (And don't forget to turn it on!) You should still take notes with pencil and paper, just in case parts of the tape are hard to hear.

2. Conduct the interview efficiently.
   - Arrive on time and be friendly and courteous.
   - Greet the person and restate the reason for the interview.
   - Ask questions one at a time. Listen carefully and take brief notes. If a response is interesting or surprising, ask the person to elaborate.
   - If you would like to use a quotation later on, make sure you copy down each word exactly. Read the statement back to the person and ask permission to use it as a direct quotation.
   - Manage your time carefully. For example, if you have thirty minutes and ten questions, do not spend fifteen minutes on the first two questions. Ask the important questions first.
   - Thank the person for his or her time.

3. Follow up immediately.
   - Write a brief letter of thanks.
   - Review your notes. Expand on what you have written while the interview is fresh in your mind. Write down your thoughts and impressions. Draw conclusions.
   - If you must phone the interview subject to clarify a point, do so as soon as possible. Phone only once.

CROSS-REFERENCE

▶ Use the model for a follow-up letter given on page 149.

Job Interviews

1. Plan carefully in advance.
   - Anticipate the interviewer's questions and try to plan responses. The table below lists some typical, general questions that you might be asked, along with some tips on how to respond.

QUESTION	SUGGESTED RESPONSES
What do you feel you have to offer this company? Why are you applying for this position?	Questions like these are designed to give you a forum to summarize your qualifications for the job. You might talk about your experience, your education, and your personality traits. Make sure you relate them all directly to the position and company in question.
Do you prefer working with other people or by yourself?	Think about which style of working is likely to be emphasized in the job you are applying for. (Hint: most jobs require both styles to some degree or another.) Answer honestly, but make sure you make it clear that you are able and willing to work both cooperatively and independently (unless you really aren't).
How do you respond to criticism?	Make it clear that you welcome constructive criticism. If possible, have ready beforehand an example of how you have used criticism to improve your performance at school or in another position. Make sure the example emphasizes the positive result rather than any less-than-perfect action that brought on the criticism.
What are your future educational plans?	Be honest, but leave the door open to future studies.
Are you willing to work overtime when necessary?	If you really won't be willing to work overtime, and the job demands it, you will probably not last long anyway. On the other hand, consider how much the job means to you. It might be worth a few extra evenings. A good compromise is to say something like "within reason."
What are your major strengths and weaknesses?	Name your weakness first, and try to make it sound as if it is really almost a strength! For example, you might say, "I think sometimes I'm too much of a perfectionist," or, "Until last year, I might have said I was afraid of public speaking, but I've been working hard at that end of things, and I think I've made great strides." Finish your answer with a description of what you think your best asset is in relation to the job.

QUESTION	SUGGESTED RESPONSES
What aspect of yourself would you like to improve?	If possible, think of an aspect of yourself that you are already in the process of improving. For example, "I am very interested in improving my computer skills, and I will be starting a computer programming course in the fall," or, "For the past three months, I have been doing volunteer work with younger children, which has really helped me improve my leadership skills."

- Be prepared to provide information about yourself. Bring anything you might need to take a test or to demonstrate your aptitude for the job.
- Make sure you know exactly how to get to the place of the interview and how long it will take to get there.

2. Make a good impression.
   - Dress neatly.
   - Be on time.
   - Be courteous and respectful but not too modest or shy.
   - Listen carefully to each question and answer it directly and concisely. Speak clearly and do not use slang or informal language.
   - Emphasize your strong points. If you don't have much working experience related to the position, stress how your other experience and qualifications will help you in the job. Your personality, enthusiasm, willingness to learn, and education may help convince the interviewer you are right for the job.
   - Ask questions about the job and the company. Be enthusiastic and appear interested, but don't try to monopolize the interview.
   - Make eye contact with your interviewer.
   - Avoid saying anything negative about previous employers, schools, etc. Accentuate the positive whenever possible.
   - Thank the person for his or her time. Make it clear that you are interested in the job, and ask when they will be making their final decision.

3. Follow up immediately.
   - Write a follow-up letter of thanks.

CROSS-REFERENCE

▶ See the sample follow-up letter on page 150.

A P P L Y   I T !

▶ *Working with a partner, role-play an interview, either for a job you intend to apply for, or for one of the following positions:*

1. A summer job as a camp counsellor.
2. A part-time job working as a receptionist in an office.
3. A summer job working for a painting company.
4. A summer job planting trees.
5. A part-time job working at a fast-food restaurant.
6. A summer job cleaning cages at the zoo.

Take turns in the role of interviewer and interviewee.

SPEECHES

Like an essay, a speech can be used to inform, explain, entertain, persuade, impress, or any combination of these. But a speech is not quite the same thing as an essay. If you have ever tried reading one of your essays out loud, you have probably found that some of the language that seems perfectly appropriate in writing sounds stilted and formal when spoken out loud. Also, it is easier to follow a logical argument in writing. When your audience is listening to a speech, they cannot cast their eye back over an earlier section to remind themselves of what was said or re-read a section they did not understand the first time.

Writing Speeches

You can use the writing process referred to in Chapter 1 to write your speech, but bear the following pointers in mind:

- Start off with a hook. You need to grab your listeners' interest right away. Otherwise, their attention may wander. Try opening with a startling statement or image, a humorous story, a personal anecdote ... anything that will make them sit up and listen. Make sure you connect your opening with the main idea you want to get across. In other words, don't just stand there and tell a joke you heard yesterday because it is funny. Find a connection.

- Give clear signposts along the way. Be sure to state clearly what you intend to talk about near the beginning of your talk, and perhaps give your listeners an indication of what points you will raise along the way. Make sure the structure of your argument is especially clear. Every so often, it is a good idea to summarize the points you have covered so far.

- Write a strong conclusion. You don't want to end your talk with "And that's it" or "That's all I have to say." Recap the main ideas, and state your conclusion in strong, simple words.

- Use vivid, concrete images. Try to find strong visual images that will stay with your audience and help them remember the gist of what you have to say. Appeal to their senses: sight, hearing, smell, taste, and touch.

- Use stories and anecdotes to illustrate difficult or important ideas.

- Keep your language simple. Unless you are giving a very formal speech, avoid using words like "therefore," "in conclusion," and "nevertheless" that you would not usually use when speaking. Avoid using too many adjectives. Instead, try to make your verbs and nouns do the work.

Here is an example of an award-winning speech written by a grade 10 student.

RACISM

"They ain't worth the land they cover and they gotta be swept off the face of this earth."

These very words were spoken by a soon-to-be leader of the Ku Klux Klan in describing visible minorities. He not only felt that he was justified in praising and promoting this opinion, but in being a part of a group that used it as an excuse to torture, degrade, and brutally murder visible minorities and religious groups. In the 1920s the KKK was the law.

1945. It is discovered that through Hitler's power, over six million Jews were tortured and put to death. All this because of his monstrous plan to attain a "master race" which he considered to be a blonde-haired, blue-eyed, white-skinned people—of which, I might add, he was not.

1963. Martin Luther King Jr. delivers his inspirational speech "I have a dream" while on the other side of the world, Nelson Mandela is sentenced to life imprisonment.

Honourable judges, ladies and gentlemen, and my fellow competitors, my topic is one that remains to be not only an obstacle in my life, but a locked door on my dreams and my future. My topic is racism.

The term racism is defined as an intolerance or hatred of other races, a preconceived, unfavourable opinion. But I know that the word "ignorance" is best-suited to describe to you exactly what racism is. And it is racial ignorance that breeds all this hatred.

I truly believe that this hatred stems from a fear deep inside all of us here today. It's a fear that all those immigrants with their "weird" clothes and accents and languages and religions and foods are going to come into OUR country and they're going to take all of OUR jobs and there'll be so many of THEM that WE will become a minority. But worse than that ... we will lose our power. So what do we do? How do we keep this from happening? Here's one way: we form a club of pure white nationalists who share this common fear. We make sure our opinions are heard and our wishes obeyed. Let's call it the Ku Klux Klan.

It all began when this little group decided to dress themselves up in white hooded sheets and prowl around in the night. The impression they sought was that they were the ghosts of the confederate dead who had arisen from the graves to wreak vengeance on an undesirable class of people—the blacks. The objective, of course, a powerful threat and a FUN game. But as their hate festered, their little game became a nightmare. They burnt the houses of previously warned blacks and beat them ruthlessly. One of their favourite forms of torture was to throw a bucket of white paint on their victim, watch as his skin tightened, his pores clogged, he suffocated and endured a long, lingering death. By 1930, there were over 500 groups belonging to the KKK.

I will not condemn these members, however, for coming together and speaking what they believe, because if my rights guarantee that I have the freedom of speech and of assembly, then they should be guaranteed those very same rights. But it terrifies me to think that there were 500 groups of people who had so much hate inside of them, that human nature makes us believe that we can only attain power by conquering and hurting other people. We cannot and should not be allowed to stop them from coming together and speaking what they believe, but I wonder—how do you stop the violence that systematically erupts?

On the other hand, it may be argued that if a black person can wear a shirt with Malcolm X on it, holding a gun in his hand, that says "by any means necessary," then why do we only condemn the KKK for keeping white supremacy alive? My answer to this is very simple. I say that whether it be black against white or white against black—if there's negativity, it's our duty to stop it.

Yet I think back to the time when Malcolm spoke his wisdom to the world and wonder if "by any means necessary" had to apply because the measures taken had to be extreme in order to accomplish any significant change. However, today we can't use any means. We must try to find an intelligent and peaceful way to stop all this negativity.

If Adolf Hitler was sitting here today, I wonder if he could come up here, look me in the eyes and justify his heartless destruction. Had he ever known a young Jewish girl such as Anne Frank, who had so much love and so many dreams, could he have killed her himself? And I think of Anne, a 13-year-old girl. She was sent to a concentration camp and treated as if she was an animal until the day that she died. How could she possibly have said "in spite of everything, I still believe people are good at heart"? And that's where I stop. I start to look for the good things, the things that Anne would see. Anne would see people like Nelson Mandela and Martin Luther King and John F. Kennedy, who have fought so hard to open some of those locked doors for me. And I know there is a difference. I see more hope than I ever did hatred.

1991. A black man by the name of Rodney King is beaten 56 times by four white police officers.

1992. Neo-Nazism resurfaces in Germany as dozens of Turkish immigrants are victimized.

1993. There are now three times as many groups belonging to the KKK as there were in 1930. That's one thousand, five hundred groups.

Three short months ago, in Toronto, students were found in the schoolyard of Riverdale Collegiate Institute passing out racial hate literature.

But before I get angry and say "things haven't changed, they're actually getting worse! I will always be judged first by the colour of my skin" I stop again. I think of what Anne would see. Anne would see that the person who filmed the Rodney King incident was *white*. Anne would see that the day after the riots in Germany, 4000 German citizens marched down the streets of Munich singing "foreigners stay, Nazis go!" Anne would see that as we educate our children, racism will be abolished and the KKK will disappear. And Anne would see that as soon as the students of Riverdale were made aware of the situation in their yard, the ENTIRE student body stormed onto that field and put an immediate end to the flyers.

And now. I would like to tell you what I see. I see a beautiful rainbow of colours before me and I see my friends. And as I look into the eyes of a group of people who are actually listening to what I have to say, I can see hope.

Maybe education and love have blinded me, but I can only see one race—the human race.

—*Tanya (Toni) DeMello*

T R Y I T !

▶ *Read the sample speech. Why do you think the speech would or would not be effective? Use the list of suggestions for writing speeches above to guide your analysis.*

Practising Your Speech

Refer to the section on *Effective Speaking* for some general hints for preparing a speech. Pay particular attention to *Step 3: Practise your delivery.*

Try not to read your speech word for word. Once it is written, read it over and over until you are very familiar with it. Then make up small 7 cm x 13 cm (3" x 5") notecards that you can refer to during the speech. Write brief notes on each card so that you can read them quickly. Here is a sample notecard for a speaker:

```
                                                    7




              Racist hatred stems from fear.



```

Use the cards to remind you of the main points you want to make. Then practise until you are comfortable using the reminders.

What To Do if You Blank Out

"The human brain is a wonderful organ. It starts to work as soon as you are born, and doesn't stop until you get up to deliver a speech."
—George Jessel

Almost everyone gets nervous when they have to speak before an audience. Your nerves will probably calm down once you get going. If you do blank out, stop for a moment and give yourself time to calm down. Take a breath, look around at the audience, take a sip of water. You might buy some time (and jog your memory) by summarizing what you have said so far. Then do the best you can by sticking to the phrases and ideas you have listed in your notes. Even if you don't end up sounding as polished as you did when you practised in front of the mirror, you will impress people with your poise.

Speaking in front of an audience can be scary. But the more you do it, the easier it becomes. Just remember to be yourself, and keep your sense of humour!

▶ *Pick one of your essays from your portfolio and practise reading it out loud as a speech. If possible, tape it. Take note of what does and doesn't sound good out loud. List ways you could adapt the essay if you had to present it as a speech.*

Announcements An announcement is a short statement designed to give information and arouse interest. It should be complete and accurate. Make sure you have all the information that you will need before you give the announcement. An announcement should include some or all of the following, depending on the subject:

- the name of the group sponsoring the event;
- the nature of the event;
- the date, time, and place of the event;
- the price of tickets and where to buy them;
- the purpose of the event;
- how the listener or reader can respond if the announcement is not about ticket sales or an event.

Here is a sample announcement:

The Women's Athletic Association is sponsoring a dance. It will be held next Friday, October 31, at 8 p.m. in the school gymnasium. Come and have a good time. Since Friday will be Halloween, the dance will be a costume party; prizes will be given for the best costumes. Tickets are $5 each and are on sale at the student council office. Remember, the dance is on Friday, October 31, at 8 p.m. in the gym. Proceeds will be used for new uniforms for the women's basketball team.

CHECKLIST FOR PUBLIC SPEAKING

Have I:

☑ Prepared an opening that will grab the audience's attention?

☑ Written a speech that is appropriate for the occasion?

☑ Used strong images that will appeal to my audience?

☑ Prepared and brought all the materials I need (note cards, illustrations, and so on)?

☑ Practised my delivery so that I feel comfortable with it?

☑ Timed my speech to make sure the length is appropriate?

MULTIMEDIA PRESENTATIONS

In a multimedia presentation, you coordinate various media (music, writing, speaking, objects, illustrations, and so on) to convey your message or idea. The advantage of using a combination of media is that you can appeal to more than one of your audience's senses. Your audience will be more stimulated, and therefore more interested in what you have to say. Here are some guidelines for combining media.

- Make sure all the technical equipment you will need is working well and that you know how to use it.

- Pay close attention to timing. Make sure you know when to move to the next slide, for example, so that the music and the images being projected move together.

- Choose your media carefully. Think about which senses you want to appeal to and what will make your subject come alive for your audience. For example, don't use a piece of music because it happens to be your favourite; consider what it will contribute to the mood or tone of the presentation.

- Try to appeal to as many senses as possible. Here are some ideas:

Sight: Posters, graphics, magazine illustrations, news articles, charts, graphs, overhead projections, lighting, scale models, maps, computer animation, computer images.

Sound: Music, sound effects tapes, taped extracts from books or speeches.

Touch: Hands-on displays, scale models, interactive computer programs.

Smell: Cooking, perfumes, (nonirritating) chemicals.

Taste: Cooking, (nonpoisonous) chemicals.

CROSS-REFERENCE

▶ For tips on how to use different types of graphs in a written or oral presentation, see page 85.

Examples of How to Use Multimedia Effectively

Here is how groups working on different science projects might use multimedia to improve the effectiveness of their presentations.

GROUP 1: *Black Holes*

You cannot touch a black hole. In fact, no one has ever seen one. In order to make the idea of a black hole real, this group decided to use a clip from a video called "A Brief History of Time" which showed a computer image of a black hole. This helped to make the concept more understandable, since it gave their audience something to visualize. In addition, they chose some futuristic background music to help establish a mood of mystery and awe as they explained their subject.

GROUP 2: *The Canadian Shield*

This group used a slide show to familiarize their audience with what the shield looked like. As well, they obtained pieces of rock from the shield itself, and allowed the audience to handle them. Finally, to help their audience appreciate the immense age of the rocks on the shield, they drew a timeline that related the formation of the shield with events in world history that their audience could relate to, such as the Big Bang, the first appearance of life on the planet, and the appearance of *Homo Sapiens*.

GROUP 3: *Animal Communication*

Group three's presentation included tape recordings of whales and dolphins, as well as a series of photographs showing monkeys who had been taught to communicate using sign language.

GROUP 4: *Smoking and Health*

This group used an interactive computer quiz to get their audience interested in finding out more. They also collected anti-smoking pamphlets and posters for distribution. Finally, they unrolled a cigarette, and used labels to indicate the contents (e.g., tar, nicotine, etc.) and the possible effects of a typical cigarette.

Making Videos

Another useful tool for multimedia presentations is a video camera. There are a few basic rules and terms you should know before you begin.

1. If possible, mount your camera on a tripod, or stand. Use a dolly (wheels that attach to the bottom of a tripod) if you want to move the camera around. Doing so will make your video look much more smooth and professional.

2. If you are using automatic focus, remember to keep whatever you want the camera to focus on in the centre of the frame.

If you are using manual focus, be sure to adjust the lens until your subject is perfectly in focus.

3. Avoid backlit shots, in which a lighting source is facing the camera. For example, if you film someone standing in front of a window, you will probably only be able to see a silhouette of the person.

4. As you compose your shots, remember that certain shapes are particularly pleasing to the eye. These are the triangle, circle, oval, S curve, and L shape. Try to arrange the elements of your picture in one of these patterns. Remember, too, that a picture with dominant horizontal lines tends to make a scene look peaceful, while vertical lines give an impression of strength, power, and endurance.

5. Watch out for things in the picture that may distract your viewers. If you want them to pay attention to the soccer game being played on the field, be sure that they are not distracted by a dog lounging off to one side.

6. Decide how broad a scene you want to portray. The field of view refers to how big a subject looks in relation to its surroundings. Your field of view can range from extreme close-up, in which the subject fills the screen, to extreme long shot, in which you include the whole setting of the scene. Generally speaking, close-ups tend to provoke more of an emotional reaction in the viewer. Long shots are useful for conveying information, such as the context, time of day, location, etc. in which the action is taking place. Viewers tend to find a medium shot, in which the subject is shown from about the waist up, to be the most comfortable, neutral field of view. This is the perspective we usually have on someone we are talking to face to face.

7. Another important factor in setting the mood of your picture is the camera angle you choose. A high camera angle, in which the camera is placed above the subject, looking down on it, tends to make the viewer feel dominant and in control. It also may tend to belittle the subject. A low camera angle, when the camera is looking up at the subject, tends to make your audience feel uncomfortable or fearful.

8. When arranging a shot, remember that the middle of the picture is the most noticeable area; the top half of the picture is more noticeable than the bottom half; and the bottom corners of the screen are the least noticeable areas of the shot.

9. Make your shots more interesting by placing the subject a little off to one side, but keep the focal point about one third in from the edges of the screen for maximum visibility.

10. Plan your transitions from one shot to another carefully. The most basic transition, and the one most frequently used, is a cut, or sudden change from one scene to another. When cutting, be sure that the second scene is shot from a different angle than the first, or a different field of view. If it is only slightly different, the scene will seem to jump and break the flow of the video.

For variety, you might try using one of the following techniques instead of a straight cut (it may take some practice to get good at some of these techniques).

- Panning: moving the camera slowly to the right or left, without actually moving your feet (or the tripod).

- Tilting: moving the camera up or down without actually moving your feet (or the tripod).

When panning or tilting, remember to move the camera much more slowly than you would normally move your head. Otherwise you are liable to end up with a blur. When you finish panning or tilting, freeze the shot for about five seconds, so your viewer can reorient himself or herself, before moving on.

- Dollying: moving closer to or further away from your subject.

- Trucking: moving slowly to the right or left of the subject.

- Arcing: moving slowly around the subject in a semicircle.

- Fading: gradually closing or opening the iris of the camera, so that the scene gradually fades into black (fade-out), or so that a scene gradually emerges from a black screen (fade-in).

- Zooming: moving from one field of view to a closer field of view by adjusting the length of the camera lens.

APPLY IT!

▶ *Before you start shooting a video, spend a few hours watching different types of television shows. Turn the sound off and pay attention to the use of field of view, transitions, and picture composition in the camera work. Do certain types of shots come up often in certain types of shows? For example, why are there so many close-ups in soap operas? Why are television reporters usually shown from the waist up? How can this information help you in planning your own video project?*

Computers and Multimedia   Computers are being used more and more in business and other multimedia demonstrations. If you have access to the equipment, and
you know how to use the programs, you can create startling effects on
a computer screen. Here is a list of possible uses of computers that
you may want to try or find out more about:

>   combining graphics (illustrations) with text;
>
>   creating graphs, charts, and tables;
>
>   creating artwork;
>
>   animation;
>
>   creating and running interactive programs;
>
>   creating and manipulating 3-D images;
>
>   presenting video clips;
>
>   altering photographs.

APPLY IT!

▶ *What types of media might you use to present information either
on one of the following subjects or on a project you are currently
working on? Take into account the materials you have available.*
The Spice Trade
Canadian Prime Ministers
Photosynthesis
Destruction of the Amazonian rainforest
The Chinese (or other) community in Canada

C H A P T E R   8

STUDY SKILLS

Living in the Age of Information means that all through your life you will need to keep up with new information and acquire new skills. Learning how to learn—developing good study habits—is one of the most important skills you can acquire. The tips contained in this chapter will help you use your time effectively, and improve your reading skills, note taking, and exam answers.

CONTENTS

MANAGING YOUR TIME

Knowing how to use the time you have available is an important skill. Here are a few tips to help you use your day effectively.

- Break large projects down into smaller tasks. It is better to plan a small task that you know you will be able to complete than to do nothing because you can't finish the whole thing in one try. If you are having trouble getting started on a history project, for instance, set yourself the task of going to the library to look up books on your topic, or plan to read through your notes to get ideas for a topic.

- Work in small blocks of time. If you are really feeling pressured, try breaking your day down into fifteen-minute segments. Studying for an exam for fifteen minutes every day is better than waiting until the day before a test and cramming.

> Strive for excellence but not perfection! Often, insisting on doing something perfectly is a way of avoiding doing it at all. Get down to it, and do the best you can with the time you have available.

CROSS-REFERENCE

▶ For other uses of lists, see *Using Lists* on page 212.

- Make lists. Get an appointment book, and keep it close by all the time. At the beginning of every week, look ahead to see what you have planned that week. Every morning, consult your appointment book, and make a list of all the things you have to do that day. As you do them, cross them off the list. If something on your list doesn't get done, don't give up. Just move it ahead to the next day.

> If you have seven things on your list and three are quick and easy, try to get the three easy things out of the way first. That will almost cut your list in half.

- Be realistic. Don't schedule study time on Friday night if you know you will want to go out with your friends then. Think about when you work best, and try to work on your most important projects at that time.

APPLY IT!

▶ *Write a list of all the tasks you have to accomplish in the next 24 hours. Look over the list and decide if there are any small tasks that you can take care of right away. Then set a schedule for accomplishing the rest of your goals. Cross each item off the list as you do it.*

READING

Francis Bacon wrote, "Some books are to be tasted, others to be swallowed, and a few to be chewed and digested." You are probably being asked to do a great deal of reading, especially for reports, essays, and exams. If you try to "chew" every morsel of every page, you will soon suffer from information indigestion. Some material only requires that you glance through it quickly, while other material demands your full concentration. Learn to tell the difference and to tailor your reading style to suit your needs.

Skimming Material

The way to get the most out of what you read in the shortest time period is to skim. This method will give you a general sense of the material you have to read and tell you whether or not the material is useful. Here's how to skim a book.

1. Start with the title. It will give you a clue to the subject matter.

2. Next, read the table of contents. It will give a preview of the specific subjects covered in the book and may list special features that could help you, such as maps, tables, or appendices.

3. Read the preface, foreword, or introduction to find out the purpose of the book.

4. Look at any appendices included at the back of the book. These contain basic reference materials that may be useful. For example, you may find a list of the prime ministers of Canada and their dates in office, a chart giving information on the planets in the solar system, and so on.

5. Check to see if there is an index. It may help you to locate a specific piece of information later.

6. Check the copyright page. It will tell you the date and place of publication. If you need up-to-date information, the date the book was published will tell you if the book is too old to be of use to you. Finding out where a book was published can also be significant. For example, if you are writing a paper on organized crime in Canada and the book was published in England, the information it contains will probably not be much help.

7. Finally, read the chapter headings and quickly flip through the pages to get the main ideas. Occasionally, read a short section that looks important. It may deal with what you really want to know.

Reading to Remember When you want to read in more depth, how do you know what parts are important to remember? How can you retain all of that information? Here are some tips to help you remember what you read.

1. Read with a purpose. If you know what you are looking for, it is much easier to remember what you read. If you are doing research for a paper, your purpose is to gather information on the topic you have chosen. However, if you do not have such an explicit reason for reading, try turning any chapter headings into questions to guide you. For example, you would read this chapter, titled *Study Skills*, by formulating a question such as, "which study skills are most useful to learn?" Do the same for each subhead within the chapter.

2. Get the big picture first. Look over all the headings in the chapter or book before you begin. Doing so will help you to get an overall sense of what the selection is about, which in turn will help you understand the details.

3. Before you start reading, ask yourself what you expect to find out. As you read, visualize the material, predict what is to come, and revise your interpretations as you go.

4. Put the information in your own words. When you have read through a section of the material, stop for a minute and try to summarize in your own words what you have just read.

To Skim or To Read? To decide how closely you need to read a particular book or article, consider the following questions:

- How much do you know about the subject? If you are just starting out and are not very familiar with the topic you are reading about, you might find skimming lightly over a few books a good way to get your bearings and get a general sense of the issues involved.

- How difficult is the subject? Books on topics you find difficult will likely require more concentration and more focused reading than subjects you find easier to understand.

- Why are you reading? If all you need to know are general details on a subject, you don't need to read a 400-page book from beginning to end. You can skim the material to find the relevant dates and events. However, if you plan to write a more detailed account, you might need to tackle the whole book. Finally, if you are only interested in one specific aspect of a larger topic, skim to find the chapters that deal with that topic, and then read those pages more slowly.

Whether you are skimming or giving a text your full concentration, always read with a purpose. Before you pick up the book, ask yourself what you hope to get out of reading it. Reading with a purpose makes it easier for your brain to distinguish important information from irrelevant details.

MAKING NOTES

Nobody's mind can keep track of all the information it receives. Notes are a good way to remember things that are important. You can take notes from many sources, including books, lectures, speeches, or films. Whatever the source, here is how to record your notes:

- At the top of the page, identify the source of information (the title of the lecture or book, including pages or sections covered) and the date the notes were written.

- Write neatly and leave space for additional information. Keep all notes for a single subject together and in order by date or topic.

- Write the ideas in your own words. This technique forces you to think about what is being said.

- Be selective. Write down only main ideas, important supporting ideas, and facts. If you try to write down every idea and example, you will probably get confused.

- Use symbols and abbreviations that will make sense to you later.

- Whenever possible, take notes in outline point form. This method organizes your material and thoughts as you go along.

CROSS-REFERENCE

▶ For specific advice on taking notes for research papers, see page 122.

Here is an example of how your notes might look for the first section of this chapter on managing your time. (Note that these hints apply to notes taken from spoken *or* written sources.)

12/12/95
COMMUNICATIONS HANDBOOK
Notes on Ch. 8: Study Skills
1. Time Mgmt.
    - Break lge projects down to <er tasks
    - Divide time into short segments (15 mins.?)
    - Don't try to do everything
    - Make lists
        - aptmt. book
        - daily list
        - do easy things first
    - Balance work/leisure times

USING LISTS

Lists are an informal method of keeping track of what you have to do and what you want to do. All lists contain a line-by-line summary of things to do or remember or get. Here are some ways you can use lists in school:

1. In the first few weeks of school, make a master list for each of your classes that describes:
   - the course requirements (number of exams, projects, essays, assignments, and how much each counts toward the final grade);
   - your teacher's special rules (write assignments in ink, points subtracted for late work, presentation requirements for papers, and so on);
   - the topics the class will cover.

   Attach each list to the inside front cover of the appropriate notebook or section in your notebook.

2. Regularly make a list of things to do, especially when you feel pressured for time. Then use the list to establish your priorities.

3. Make a list of questions to ask your teacher if you are not sure about an assignment or are particularly interested in it.

4. Keep a list of words that you often misspell or confuse. Refer to this list whenever you are revising or editing a paper or assignment.

EXAMINATIONS

Studying for the Exam

Here are some guidelines to help you prepare for an exam. Many of them apply to study habits in general.

1. Choose a regular place and time for studying. The place should be quiet and comfortable (not the TV room). Choose the time carefully so that your other activities will not interfere. Take regular breaks but keep them short.

2. Start studying for an exam several days before the date it is scheduled. Then review the material again the evening before. This plan will give you time to find out about something you don't know and makes the night before a lot less frantic.

3. While you study, note the main ideas and organize the details and examples under these ideas. Also, make note of any questions you have that will need to be answered before the exam.

4. Select a number of potential exam questions and practise answering them in outline form. Then choose one question and write a full answer for it.

Writing the Exam

Exams come in all types and sizes. You've probably experienced quite a few of these already. Here are some guidelines that apply equally to all types of exams, from multiple choice and true-false questions to essay-style questions and problems.

1. Make a quick survey of the entire exam.

2. Note any specific directions, such as "Write on one side of the paper only," or "Do all scratch work on the exam paper."

3. Take note of each section in the exam, how many points each is worth, which sections you can do quickly, and which will take more time.

4. Figure out how much time you have to complete the exam, and then allot a portion of that time to each section. Write your time allocations in the margin beside each section heading.

5. Do the easy sections of the exam first. If you don't know an answer, or think it will take you a long time, go on to the next question. Then return to the first question later.

6. Write neatly and clearly. A "T" that looks like an "F" in a true-false section will cost you marks.

7. Identify precisely what the question is asking and answer accordingly. If the question asks, "What is the quotient of 752.8 divided by 27.62, rounded off to the nearest hundredth?" you won't get full marks for simply performing the calculation. You need to remember to round off your answer as well.

8. Check over your completed exam. Make sure you have answered everything that you can. Look for grammar, punctuation, spelling, arithmetic errors, and any words that are hard to read because you were writing fast. Write your name on each page.

Essay-Style Questions

When writing essay-style answers to exam questions, it is tempting to launch right in to the writing without any preparation to be sure you get all the information down on paper. But a few minutes spent organizing your ideas can mean the difference between mediocrity and excellence. Here is how to approach essay-style questions:

CROSS-REFERENCE

▶ Study the list of key words on page 95.

1. Look for key words in the question, such as explain, compare, contrast, discuss, and define.

2. Spend a few moments gathering your thoughts. On scrap paper, list what you know and write a brief outline, cluster, or tree diagram before you start writing.

3. Use a formal writing style for your answers. Unless told otherwise, always write in full sentences.

4. Your opening statement should be a thesis statement. Summarize the main points you intend to make in the introduction; that way, if you do not have time to finish, your teacher will at least know what you intended to write. In the paragraphs that follow, concentrate on elaborating each main point; keep your supporting details simple and concise.

5. Watch out for spelling and punctuation errors. If you have no idea how to spell a word that comes to mind, avoid using it; think of another word to replace it.

Multiple Choice Questions

Here are some tips for taking multiple choice tests.

• Read the instructions carefully to find out if you are looking for the *right* answer or the *best* answer. In the first case, all the other answers will be at least partly wrong. In the second case, any or all of the choices may be right; your task is to evaluate which is the *most* accurate.

• Look over *all* the answers before choosing one.

• Narrow your choices: cross out all answers that are obviously incorrect.

• Watch out for negatives: it is easy to overlook words like "not," "never," and "don't" that change the meaning of the question completely. (If the statement contains strong positive words like "always" and "forever," be careful that the answer you choose is not just true sometimes or for a while.)

• When in doubt, stick with your first answer. Don't change an answer unless you are absolutely sure it is wrong.

ANSWERS TO TRY IT EXERCISES

CHAPTER 1 ▶ **DRAFTING,** *PAGE 15*
Answers will vary.

TREE DIAGRAMS, *PAGE 16*
Answers will vary.

CHAPTER 2 ▶ **TRANSITIONS,** *PAGE 33*
[NOTE: Other answers are possible.]

1. Care for a crisp, juicy grasshopper for breakfast? In many parts of the world, **insects are** considered perfectly acceptable to eat.

2. **Although** North American culture is revolted by the thought of eating bugs, locusts, grasshoppers, ants, and bees are considered delicacies by some people.

3. Even stinkbugs are eaten and enjoyed in some parts of the world, **although their** glands contain cyanide, which is poisonous.

4. Why do some societies eat insects? For one thing, they are an abundant protein source. Areas like the rainforest do not have many **sources of protein,** since there is no room to plant crops and large animals are hard to come by.

5. The real question is not "Why do some people eat insects?" **The real question is,** "Why does our culture *not* think of insects as food?"

6. We gladly devour crab and lobster, in spite of their insect-like appearance. Why do we consider **insects** taboo?

SENTENCE VARIETY, *PAGE 35*
[NOTE: Other answers may also be correct.]

The Jim twins are twin brothers **who** were separated at birth. **They were** adopted into different families, **and each was named** James by his adoptive parents. **When** the **two Jameses** were reunited at the age of thirty-nine, a string of astonishing similarities was discovered in their lives. Both had been married to women named Linda **and** remarried women named Betty. Jim Springer had a son named James Allan, **while Jim Lewis had a son named James Alan. Each brother had an** adopted brother named Larry, **and each had** named a pet dog Toy. Both brothers had been part-time deputy sheriffs in the state of Ohio. Both had driven a Chevrolet from Ohio to the same **three-block long** place in Florida. Both brothers are six feet tall, weigh 180 pounds, **and** suffer from tension headaches **which** started when they were 18 years old. Both did mechanical drawing, used block lettering, **and liked** carpentry.

SENTENCE FRAGMENTS, *PAGE 36*

1. **Fragments:**
   Bugs, dirt, poison ivy.
   Eating soggy sandwiches.
   The strawberries squashed at the bottom of the basket.
   No dishes to clean, no pots to scrub.
   Bugs rarely in evidence.
   If you *want* fresh air.
   So.

2. **Suggested Revision:**
   Picnics are no fun. **They mean** bugs, dirt, and poison ivy, eating soggy sandwiches, and strawberries squashed at the bottom of the basket. Wouldn't you really prefer a civilized meal in a civilized restaurant, where all the cooking is done for you? **There are** no dishes to clean and no pots to scrub, **and** bugs **are** rarely in evidence. You can always open a window to get a dose of fresh air, **if** you *want* fresh air. I prefer air conditioning. So, next time someone suggests a picnic, take my advice: run!

RUN-ON SENTENCES, *PAGE 37*

Alberta singer k.d. lang caused quite a furor when she appeared in a commercial proclaiming that "meat stinks." **S**he offended a lot of people in the province who depend on cattle for their livelihood. Some animal rights activists would agree with lang. **T**hey feel that killing animals for food is immoral. Others believe that although we must protect animals from cruel treatment, it is all right to eat meat. These same moderates also tend to believe that using animals in research is sometimes justified; **h**owever, the hard-liners oppose any such use. Some radical activists have turned to violence to make their point, bombing meat markets and breaking into labs to free animals.

DANGLING AND MISPLACED MODIFIERS, *PAGE 38*

On December 6, 1917, two ships **called the *Mont Blanc* and the *Imo*,** collided in Halifax Harbour. The *Mont Blanc's* cargo of highly explosive materials, **including picric acid, TNT, and benzene,** caught fire and drifted in toward Halifax's north shore. At 9:06 a.m., the ship blew up, producing the largest artificial explosion the world has ever seen, except for the bombing of Hiroshima. Disintegrating into a shower of metal fragments, **the vessel caused horrific destruction.** Rescue crews found a gun from the *Mont Blanc* **that had been hurled five-and-a-half**

kilometres, embedded in the ground at Armbro Lake. **In the north end of the city**, all houses were either flattened by the blast or burned. Out of a total population of 50 000 people, 9600, or **almost** one-fifth, were killed or injured. Twenty thousand people were left with inadequate shelter **in the middle of a blizzard**, and 6000 were left **completely** homeless for several days after the explosion.

AWKWARD SENTENCES, *PAGE 39*
[NOTE: Other answers are possible.]

Hippocrates was a Greek philosopher who lived in the fifth century. As a way of explaining temperament, he developed the theory of the four humours, or fluids, namely: blood, yellow bile, black bile, and phlegm. According to Hippocrates, when an individual tended to be too sanguine, or overconfident, he or she had an excess of blood, or *sanguis*. Similarly, too much yellow bile made one quick to anger, while black bile produced melancholy, and phlegm tended to make one slow and apathetic. For many years, modern researchers dismissed Hippocrates' theory, along with all theories of personality that claim nature or biology as a major influence. They claimed that nurture was a much greater factor in determining personality. However, some are now re-examining the idea that we are born with a tendency to a particular temperament, and are proposing personality types linked to the level of naturally occurring hormones in the body. For example, where Hippocrates believed that brave, outgoing individuals had an excess of blood, some scientists have discovered that these individuals have high levels of serotonin in their bodies. Those the ancients would have called "choleric," or having an excess of yellow bile, have much lower levels of serotonin.

FAULTY PARALLELISM, *PAGE 40*
[NOTE: Other answers are possible.]

I once babysat for a real troublemaker: a three-year-old boy who had blond hair **and** an angelic smile, and **who was** used to getting his own way. As soon as his parents left, he would cry, scream, and **throw** himself on the couch. The only way to calm him down was to give him food, read him a story, or **let** him watch TV. Once he disappeared while he was supposed to be watching cartoons. I called his name **and** ran all over the house, **but was** unable to find him. At last he sauntered into the living room calmly, **innocently**, and triumphantly, just as I was picking up the phone to call the police. He never told me where he had been; I never told his parents he was missing; and they never did understand why from then on I was always busy when they asked me to babysit!

SUBJECT-VERB AGREEMENT, *PAGE 42*
Mathematics **is** a lot easier when you have a computer or calculator in front of you. But not everyone **needs** this kind of help; mathemati-

cal prodigies turn up every so often who can mentally calculate sums that even electronic instruments **find** challenging. Some of them **claim** to see the numbers, while other prodigies associate numbers with sounds; furthermore, most **calculate** from left to right, rather than right to left as we are usually taught. One of the greatest among recent prodigies **is** a woman called Shakuntala Devi, who has toured the world demonstrating her remarkable ability. (Unfortunately, neither your pocket calculator nor Ms. Devi **is** allowed at your desk during the math exam.)

PASSIVE VOICE, *PAGE 45*
Lacrosse has several claims to distinction: it may be the oldest field sport in existence; it is certainly the oldest team sport played in North America; and, in 1760, Chief Pontiac and the Ottawas **used it** as a secret weapon in a surprise attack on Fort Michilimackinac! It seems **Pontiac's men organized** a game of *baggataway* (the original Native name for what we now call lacrosse) directly outside the gates of the impenetrable garrison. The **unfamiliar sport intrigued the** soldiers inside the fort, so **they opened** the gates, and stood at a distance, watching the play. At one point, **one of the players shot** the ball toward the gate and **the rest of the two teams chased it**. Before the garrison soldiers were aware of what was happening, **Pontiac's men brought** weapons out of their hiding places, and **stormed** the gate.

PRONOUNS, *PAGE 49*
My crazy uncle Herbert told my sister and **me** about the Tichborne Affair when we were children, but **she** and I only found out recently that the incident really happened. Here is how the story goes: When rich young Roger Tichborne is lost at sea in 1854, his mother, **who** is heartbroken, puts ads in newspapers around the world, in hopes of finding him alive. Eleven years later, lo and behold, someone from Australia **answers** the ad!

The man **who** appears on Lady Tichborne's doorstep, claiming to be heir to the family fortune, is not very convincing to those who knew **Roger** well. Most **dismiss** him as a fraud, but none **has** counted on the strength of Lady Tichborne's self-deception. Young Roger was slim, had straight dark hair and a tattoo on his right arm, and could speak French fluently, but none of these traits **appear** in **the claimant**. In fact, the claimant is grossly overweight, has wavy blond hair, does not have a tattoo, knows not a word of French, and speaks fondly of a grandfather **whom** the young Roger never met!

In spite of this, Arthur Orton almost succeeded in claiming Roger Tichborne's inheritance, thanks to the support of **Roger's** doting mother. It was **she** who championed **Orton's** cause more than anyone—although Orton did eventually manage to convince dozens of people to testify in court that he was the rightful heir. In the end, Lady Tichborne died, leaving Orton without support, and he was jailed for

14 years. Orton only confessed his deception years later when, penniless, he sold his story to a magazine for £3000.

CLICHES, *PAGE 56*
Answers will vary.

CHAPTER 3

HYPHENS, *PAGE 67*
The Treetops Hotel is a very **well-known** tourist attraction in Kenya. This **five-metre-high** hotel is built in a mgumu tree, right beside an **all-important** watering hole for animals. In the past, the **well-heeled** patrons of the hotel have included the **twenty-six-year-old** daughter of King George VI, Elizabeth, along with the King's **son-in-law**, Philip. Elizabeth received the news of her father's death and her own ascension to the throne while staying at Treetops.

Be sure not to miss the **late-afternoon check-in time**; afterward, the stairs to the hotel are raised and, as the sun goes down, you can watch animals come out to drink at the pond below. But be careful: leaving your window even halfway open could mean that badly behaved monkeys will sneak in and steal the shiny necklace you inherited from your **great-grandmother**!

CAPITALIZATION, *PAGE 73*
"The **C**anadian," wrote **J. B. P**riestley in his introduction to *The Bodley Head Leacock*, "is often a baffled man because he feels different from his **B**ritish kindred and his **A**merican neighbours, sharply refuses to be lumped together with either of them, yet cannot make plain the difference." My mother is a **M**uslim, born in **P**akistan; **D**ad is a **J**ewish rabbi, born in **I**srael; **I** was born in **N**ormal, **O**hio; and we are all proud to call ourselves **C**anadian. I have noticed that **C**anadian patriotism is not usually expressed as allegiance to a flag, or to the **C**onstitution, as it is by **A**mericans. But every winter, we remember what draws us together, from north to south and east to west: the cold!

APOSTROPHES, *PAGE 78*
Have you ever had the urge to cut your hair after breaking up with someone or before turning over a new leaf? **It's** a common way to express either a new beginning or a renunciation of something. In fact, in most cultures, hair is a symbol of power, intellect, and the life force.

Think about it: why is a **soldier's** hair cut so short when he enlists? What do **monks'** tonsures signify? Why was the **sixties'** style of long hair considered so rebellious? What does a **skinhead's** baldness symbolize?

In the Old Testament story of Samson and Delilah, **Samson's** hair gives him superhuman strength—until Delilah cuts it off. In Greek mythology, **Medusa's** hair is made of snakes. One look at her and you turned to stone; **that's** what you call a bad hair day.

Answers will vary.

CHAPTER 5 ▶ PLAGIARISM, *PAGE 134*

1. Since the 1960s, one of the most controversial areas of linguistics has been the question of how we learn language. Linguist Noam Chomsky has been at the centre of the debate for decades. His view, that we are born with the ability to learn language, "has so dominated this field since the late fifties that while normally you'd describe a debate like this as having two sides, his and the other's, somehow in this case it seems that Chomsky is at the centre, with all other points of view swirling around him" **(Ingram 130)**.

   There are 150 medicine wheels still intact in North America, mostly located in southern Alberta and Saskatchewan. Montana and Wyoming also have some examples. The wheels were used for different purposes, such as **honouring those who had died, intimidating hostile bands, and serving as a focal point for religious ceremonies (Nikiforuk 51-52)**.

   OR

   There are 150 medicine wheels still intact in North America, mostly located in southern Alberta and Saskatchewan. Montana and Wyoming also have some examples. The wheels were used for different purposes, such as **"commemorating the dead, frightening away enemies . . . and anchoring spiritual observances" (Nikiforuk 51-52)**.

2. Suggested Paraphrase [NOTE: Other answers are possible.]

   Southwestern British Columbia is more prone to earthquakes than any other part of Canada. Every year, over 300 quakes shake the region. Although most of these quakes are very minor, and rarely cause damage, "history records a structurally damaging earthquake about every 25 to 45 years." Recently, scientists have come to believe that the region has weathered on average at least one massive earthquake every thousand years or so for the last 7000 years, and that a truly cataclysmic quake could rock the area again at any time (Tempelman-Kluit 78).

CHAPTER 7 ▶ SPEECHES, *PAGE 200*
Answers will vary.